Darwin's Fox and My Coyote

Darwin's Fox and My Coyote

HOLLY MENINO

UNIVERSITY OF VIRGINIA PRESS
CHARLOTTESVILLE

University of Virginia Press
© 2008 by Holly Menino
Printed in the United States of America on acid-free paper

First published 2008

9 8 7 6 5 4 3 2 1

LIBRARY OF CONGRESS CATALOGING-IN-PUBLICATION DATA

Menino, H. M.
   Darwin's fox and my coyote / Holly Menino.
      p.   cm.
   Includes bibliographical references.
   ISBN 978-0-8139-2675-9 (cloth : alk. paper)
   1. Canidae. 2. Canidae—Conservation. I. Title.
   QL737.C22M47 2008
   333.95′416—dc22
                                    2007018938

For Betty and Herb Bailey,
with love

And the Lord said unto Noah,
Come thou and all thy house
into the ark for thee have I seen
righteous before me in this generation.

Of every clean beast thou shalt
Take to thee by sevens, the male and his female: and of
     beasts that are
Not clean by two, the male and his female.

Of fowls also of the air by sevens,
the male and the female; to keep seed
alive upon the face of all the earth.

—Genesis 7:1–3

Contents

1 ⟨ Here's Where I Ride Up to It

EARLY ON A SUMMER MORNING IN UPSTATE NEW YORK, I WAS riding through a friend's farm on her horse and was headed back to the barn when I met the coyote in a hayfield. At first I thought it was a dog, just a scrawny gray shepherd. But the face was too sharp, the scrawniness was really leanness, and the animal's awareness was keener than a dog's. It was too wild for a dog. A dead rabbit hung in its jaws. I had interrupted the animal returning from a hunt.

The hay was tall, timothy just heading out and ready to be cut, and it carried a load of dew. The coyote had come fifty yards through it from the woods. It was wet across its flanks and belly. It stood gazing at me and the big, gray horse, unafraid. After a moment it put down the rabbit. The coyote's eyes were yellow, and in the early brightness the pupils looked nearly vertical. Its interest in the horse and me was frank. It was sizing up the centaur, assessing the possibilities, perhaps of food. Standing over the dead rabbit, the coyote was provocative. I knew coyotes had been spotted in the area, but I had never seen one. Now suddenly close to the animal I had the reactions that most people who confront large predators report. I was impressed by the coyote's intensity, prowess, nonchalance about killing—and I wondered momentarily if coyote killing was in some way related to human carnage. Then I was startled to realize how near it and maybe its family had been that morning and maybe on all my rides. The coyotes were there. I just wasn't paying attention.

When the horse took a step toward it, the coyote decided on the rabbit. It casually retrieved the limp carcass and set out nonchalantly for the hedgerow on the other side of the hayfield. The high grass closed over its back, and I thought, "What is this animal *doing* here?"

Little did I know that this question is central to the natural history of animals—the study of animals in their wild homes, how they manage to stay alive and reproduce, and how they are related to other animals. It's an old question among scientists, old even by the time it fueled Charles Darwin's investigations during the voyage of the *Beagle*. He understood that the answers to the question would not be simple, and he was satisfied for starters with a few spare facts or maybe just a specimen. Of course, What is this animal doing here? is really a series of interlocking questions about food, sex, reproduction, social relations, allies and enemies, survival—and land underlies the answers to all of them.

Although I didn't know this coyote would eventually lead me to Darwin, at the moment I rode up to the coyote I too would have been satisfied by a few simple, easily observed facts. I wasn't bothered by complexity of any sort. I wasn't thinking about natural history or the study of animals or the preciousness of the piece of land on which the coyote stood. I just wanted to see a little more of the animal, and I tried to follow it on horseback. But within yards, it eluded me. I rode back to the barn with no more information than the sight of the coyote had provided. I asked one of the men who worked on the farm if he had ever seen a coyote on the place. Yeah, one when he was cutting hay, and he'd seen two of them trotting along the hedgerow together. Must have been a pair.

The next day I rode out on the gray a little earlier, thinking that if the coyotes kept some kind of schedule I would see one before its hunting was finished. But maybe the day was too bright and clear. Maybe I had scared off the coyote. I tried similar strategies with small variations over the weeks I exercised the horse. But there was no repeat encounter. Later in the summer, I looked out the kitchen window over the lawn to a field on our farm where soybeans grew in narrow, bushy rows. Between two rows of beans something gray-brown slipped toward the woods. Just the back showed, like the dorsal fin of a fish. At the headlands that border the woods, it mingled with the color of the dirt and vanished.

"Did you hear the coyotes last night?" my husband asked. I hadn't. I had been up in the night and wandered out on the porch, and the night was perfectly still. But he had heard them earlier. They were not that far from us. Maybe only as far as the deep ravine in our twenty-acre patch of woods.

When the leaves were off the trees, I began to see a shape at the edge of the woods in the early mornings. Sometimes it simply appeared for a moment in the opening where the headlands of the field met the trail into the woods. Other mornings it slipped across in front of the trees and then sank into the hedgerow. There were tracks in the muddy trailhead. I had been seeing similar tracks for a year or so, but I assumed they had been made by a large dog.

That winter I found the carcass of a woodchuck near the center of the woods and far from the edge of the field where the woodchuck denned and usually did its foraging. It was a big one but not fat because it had been denned up against the cold, and it lay sprawled where it had been dropped in the snow. It was intact, its pelt unpunctured, except around its neck, which had been broken. The snow cover in the woods was old and patchy. The only identifiable tracks were those of a deer a few yards away. The next morning the carcass was in the same place, but it had been cleaned down to the skeleton, except for its head, which was still fully dressed with hair and eyes and leathery nose.

The land around our farm is not wilderness, just fields and spare woodlots that run from the highway down to the lake road, where big houses and summer cottages take over. But evidently it was wilderness enough for a big predator. The coyotes were out there taking care of coyote business in an alternate, parallel world. I wasn't getting any closer to that world. Aside from the woodchuck carcass, I had no more information than I had when I encountered the first coyote in the hayfield. Our neighbors were not long on sympathy for coyotes, and most of the people I questioned seemed to find it odd or irrelevant that I was so keen for information.

But preoccupation with one animal or another is something habitual for me, and this began as early as I can remember. As a toddler I saw no need to speak until an animal caused me to. Like Graham Greene, I have a very early memory of a dog. His memory was of a dead beagle, mine was of a sweet-natured Airedale bitch. A few weeks earlier my mother had presented me with my very first memory, a black-haired infant sister, red, slightly sticky all over, and a real squaller. Abby was not like this. She was very soft—I'm sure her coat would never pass breed standards today—and easy to get a grip on. Her eyes were a warm, solid black and as round as jack balls. I remember sitting in my high chair with this dog beside it. My mother was talking to me, and I realized indignantly that she was speaking to me as if I were a baby—I couldn't talk yet, so how else was she to treat me? But Abby did not condescend. We were colleagues, nose to nose, and so close that it troubled me that the dog had to be left behind when the family drove East to visit my grandparents. It was explained to me that Abby had some kind of ailment—what I now suspect was a miscarriage—but she would be better when we got back. Her place on the back seat of the car was empty, and after riding a couple hundred miles without her, I finally spoke. My first words were to accuse the powers in the front seat: "Abby home sick."

This sense of vital connection has continued into my adulthood. Animals are still extremely important to me, not for what they might reveal about the human species but for their own living particulars. Their experiences of life on earth are qualitatively different from our own and distinct from each other, and in these differences their lives are valuable. Animals are linked to our species through *anima*—soul, movement—and close knowledge of animals seems an essential of being human. But I am aware that my attitudes are not universal. Sadly, many people think of their pet dog or cat either as a person in a fur coat or as a kind of animated object. For them, animals exist only as extensions of themselves or as possessions. To me, it seems more useful to recognize the differences among the physical and perceptual capacities of animals, including us.

At the time I rode up to the coyote, I had, along with this philosophy, a high opinion of my understanding of animals. This was based on my experiences with domestic animals. I could look at a dog and tell you whether its agitation was anxiety or anticipation. I could watch the ears of a horse and tell you if it was about to bolt or strike with a hoof. But the coyote was a different story. The animal had no reason to have any truck with humans. It was hard to spot and even more difficult to observe. I would have no opportunity to observe it, let alone read its intentions or needs.

At this point I did what most of my readers would do. I turned to science for answers. This was fairly automatic, because for a number of years I had been interviewing scientists for radio programs on nature and the environment. I knew which floor of the university library to head for and which section of the stacks, carnivore biology.

The order Carnivora, a large and diverse group of mammals, consists, at last count, of some 271 species. What qualifies a mammal for membership in Carnivora is not, as most of us tend to assume, an exclusive diet of meat. It is ownership of a set of four teeth, two pairs of jagged premolars, matched uppers against lowers. These are the carnassials that biology texts love to refer to as "flesh-shearing" teeth, tools that appeared at some period during the animal's evolution and may or may not still be used for that purpose. There are many carnivores that are fairly ecumenical in their foraging, and a few never eat meat or even insects. In some carnivores like the fruit-eating kinkajou or the panda, which doesn't eat much flesh, the carnassials have evolved with further refinements. The carnassials of the giant panda are shaped to grind as well as slash, for instance, and on the upper carnassials of the kinkajou there is a vertical groove whose function is at the moment mysterious. The carnassials of coyotes are unremarkable in that they have retained their flesh-shearing shape, but their owners, like Aesop's fox with its bunch of grapes, have shown a willingness to sink them into any number of nonmeat items that may come to hand.

On a couple of shelves in the carnivore section, I found works on the family Canidae. Here I learned something about the coyote in the hayfield: it had arrived upstate fairly recently; it liked scrubland and open fields broken by brush and hedgerows; it used a variety of animals and plant stuff as food but strongly preferred snowshoe hare when that was on offer; it might or might not form social groups. In all these things, in everything, the coyote was, above all, most adaptable, and for this virtue, it was often referred to as a weed species.

That should have been that. But I had stayed too long in this part of the library. I knew about many of the scientists whose work stood on these several yards of utilitarian shelving. I had read George Schaller's research on lions in the Serengeti and the panda in China, Hans Kruuk on hyenas and otters, David Mech on wolves, and Alan Rabinowitz on the jaguar in Belize and the wild cats of Southeast Asia. There were many more: starting with the early surveys after World War II, biologists had been reporting from the field for popular as well as scientific audiences on an ever-wider circle of fauna: tigers in the Punjab, African hunting dogs in Kruger National Park in South Africa, foxes in Oxford, England, wolves in Minnesota, grizzlies in Yellowstone, bats, amphibians, reptiles, insects. In each case, the writer had managed to locate the animal in its singular world and to describe its existence.

These were some of the works that had propelled the nascent conservation movement of the 1960s and 1970s. Because of them, it became widely recognized and publicly articulated that animals and plants and natural areas were vulnerable. Animals that were hunted to depletion or simply pushed out of the places that sustained them would never come back. Plants chopped down at great speed or bulldozed out were unlikely to reemerge. Land taken over by humans was difficult, often impossible, to reclaim for nature, and, as Will Rogers pointed out, "they aren't making any more of it." This line of thinking has now gone deeper to include concern about losses of genes and collections of genes. The natural world is diminishing. It needs more vigilant safeguarding. People, a phenomenon after all of nature, have become the primary threat to it. To defend nature what we need to do is protect ourselves against ourselves.

Like everyone who grew up after World War II, I came of age with the conservation movement and understood that science was the wheel that drove it. About the time I was nose to nose with the Airedale, the International Union for the Protection of Nature (now called IUCN–The World Conservation Union) was founded. When I entered kindergarten, George Schaller was undertaking his first field research. During a period of gender confusion in which I was sent home from the otherwise all-boy fifth grade for fighting, the Wildlife Conservation Society, then the New York Zoological Society, began sponsoring surveys to assess the condition of wildlife in Africa and Asia. In my first year in high school, the World Wildlife Fund was established, and Rachel Carson published *Silent Spring*. Then, in 1973, while I was tending two toddlers, the Endangered Species Act was passed. This was the breaking of the wave, and it had profound effects on the ways in which people, including scientists themselves, thought about the natural world. A quarter century later, I surveyed the works of carnivore biologists and realized that the accomplishments of the conservation movement had been with me so long that I took them for granted. My attitudes were as routine as breathing, and I was all too content to let science and scientists carry the responsibility for what happened next to animals in the wild.

Conservation biologists have become the keepers of the present-day Ark, a small craft bobbing on rapidly rising waters of environmental change. They are the people we rely on to monitor the wildernesses and the world's oceans. Their job is to gather information because in terms of animal conservation, information is a wild species' first line of defense. You can protect an animal only if you know it exists and if you know what essentials keep it alive—only if you know with great specificity "what this animal is doing here." Information is what it takes to bring an animal on board to ride out the Flood. I assumed that science was adequate to this task, but I had no idea how wildlife scientists got their information. I was an amateur, in the first sense of that word, an ardent devotee with no professional training or credentials.

Riding up to the coyote, I had come face-to-face with my own ignorance. The coyote and his kind remained elusive because I didn't know how to get at the basic facts of coyote existence. I was frustrated with coyote watching, and I could see that I was—to keep this Ark metaphor going a little longer—missing the boat. At the beginning what I wanted to do was very simple. I wanted to learn how to see a wild animal the way a scientist sees it, and I was particularly interested in animals in the dog family. This was not only a matter of unfinished coyote business, but I thought dogs would be familiar and easily understood by almost anyone. I myself had a good deal of experience with dogs, and I already knew a lot of what there was to know. Or so I thought.

I planned to find a couple of scientists working in wild places on a couple of different wild animals and travel along with them, hitchhiking on the Ark. I could share their detailed observations of the animals, and maybe some of their knowledge would rub off on me. Although it hurts to admit this, my attitude was not that far removed from those of the tourists who ride in safari jeeps. It was all about seeing the animals. What could be more straightforward?

This was not the way the adventure played out, because traveling with wildlife scientists offered little opportunity to see the animals, and no opportunity at all to observe more than one animal at the same time. Instead, what I witnessed in my travels in California, New York, Chile, and Panama was the process of writing the natural history of an animal. I learned how science specifies the question, What is this animal doing here? I learned how it pinpoints what a wild animal needs and how it measures the urgency of forces like space and food and social contact. These were important lessons because, although scientists routinely explain these factors to each other, most people outside science, including avid amateurs like me, have little understanding of the interplay of the elements of animal survival. But if you care about wild animals and believe you are an advocate for their survival, you need to know how things work in the woods. That is why I consider at such length the issues of food, territory, communication, and family relations.

While it may seem unnecessary to point this out, all these animal necessities depend on the availability of land, both space and place. But for those readers whose lives roll out comfortably within the confines of apartments, office buildings, and streets and who may follow the trajectories of their jobs from one coast to the other, I want to make it clear that you cannot consider animal necessities without taking land into account. You cannot think about what a wild animal eats, how it lets its intentions be known, or how it carries out its social and sexual roles without understanding how each of these factors is anchored to land. It is often pointed out that land is shifting out from under wild animals. Their territories are crumbling at the edges, fracturing through their cores. I saw this happening on an island preserve in California, in the upstate New York pine barrens, in the Chilean cordillera, and even in the fields and lakeshore neighboring our farm.

I also learned that field research is time-consuming. It is slow and tedious, and I began to see how the slow pace of the research process can be an obstacle to conservation. Field biology spearheaded the animal conservation movement by creating a new awareness of wild animals and bringing to public consciousness the needs and vulnerabilities of these animals. It is still doing that work with the same mission, but traveling with biologists made clear to me that the process of gathering information about wildlife is too deliberate to keep pace with rapid changes to the animals' environments. I wondered what this meant about the responsibilities of amateurs, people like me.

Now I am running ahead of my story, which after all began with the coyote and his kind, animals in the order Carnivora and the family Canidae. What I needed to do was to find a couple of scientists. I wanted scientists who had projects under way and would be open to having me tag along. I wanted to get to know them, their work, and their animals. I started with senior scientists who would have the experience and perspective on current research to point out likely candidates for the project. John Gittleman, an expert in the comparative evolution of carnivores, fielded my first inquiries. Gittleman is a courtly, politic man who, because of the comparative aspect of his work, knows everybody who studies carnivores, and he guided my first contacts. I learned quickly that because field research is often a requirement for the Ph.D., good guides were most likely to be new biologists about to fledge from doctoral programs.

Todd Fuller, a senior biologist based at the University of Massachusetts, had quite a number of protégés doing fieldwork—on everything from opossums in western Massachusetts to jaguars in Costa Rica, bobcats in the West, and snow leopards in Mongolia. Elise McMahon was one of Fuller's students and had begun fieldwork in Chile, where she was trapping and tracking a rare fox called the Darwin's fox.

I contacted Elise and then drove out to Amherst. I found her on crutches, swinging along the slushy sidewalks at a good speed. There was an enormous clutch of keys in one of the hands that gripped the crutches and a shopping bag in the other. Quite independent and getting around handily on just one leg, she was in her thirties and pretty, with pale skin and a thick bob of dark hair. She wore loose trousers and a loose fleece shirt, and so far as I can remember, that describes what she wore every time I saw her.

It was a first encounter, but our talk covered a surprising range of subjects. It mixed the South American fox with films and graduate school, her dog and horses with gender issues. Elise seemed to enjoy what was hip, and she had an offhand manner that belied any difficulty in her work. The broken ankle was the result of a riding accident in Chile, and it had forced her to leave South America early and sit out the rest of the season. She was eager to go back, and she was quite willing to have me tag along. "No problem," she said. "It isn't hard to get to Chile, and we can figure out where to meet up."

It was done. The arrangements were made that simply. Nine months later, in January, I would join her in Chile, where it would be summer.

I was a little surprised that she was just as nonchalant about the rareness of her fox as she was about having an observer in Chile. True, she said, without seeming to make much of it, the Darwin's was rare. There were fewer than six hundred in the world, and all of these lived in Chile. I thought, *Rare,* how cool. I have since learned that biologists think differently about rareness than do the untrained. Rareness is important for whatever it indicates about the animal and the place it lives. But it is not glamorous, and it does not necessarily privilege one research subject over the next. I was not aware of this or of any of the other differences in the way she thought about animals and the way I thought about them. Maybe I should have had some premonition of these differences, but then Elise hadn't troubled herself much about the new ways of thinking she would encounter when she entered science.

"What made you want to do something like this?" I asked.

"I was in Germany doing graduate work in comparative literature, film studies. And I saw this movie. It was about Dian Fossey." Something about Fossey's work with gorillas moved her. Something clicked. "I said, '*I* could do that!'" I found this comment comforting. My own background hardly suited me for the experiences ahead of me, and I was reassured by the thought that she had been able to transform her intellectual pursuits so radically.

Enlisting Elise had not been difficult. But I needed a second guide, not so much to compare the scientists and their ideas as to look at a different animal living in a different situation. When I visited John Gittleman in Charlottesville, he pointed out something that now seems quite obvious to me: "You know, the big carnivores, the charismatic animals, have been *done.* A good many people have worked on them. But there are lots of animals in the middle of the system that we know nothing about." He happened to have on his desk a dissertation he had recently supervised on kinkajous. It was written by someone named Roland Kays. "You could have some fun with this," he promised.

Roland was doing postdoctoral work at the Field Museum in Chicago, but it was a while before I could meet him in person. He was on his way to Peru and a fast-sweep wildlife survey. After that, he told me, his postdoc would end and he would be taking a new job. In Albany, New York, he said casually, where he would be curator of mammals for the state museum. He would need to do some kind of research on upstate mammals, and coyotes, he said, seemed like a good possibility. Maybe Roland Kays would be a ticket back to my coyote, and a coyote project could make an interesting pairing with the Darwin's fox research. Both animals were canids, members of the dog family. One was thriving, colonizing the fringes of the suburbs, and the other trying to hold its own in a remote South American forest.

Keep in touch, Roland suggested. It wouldn't be difficult to get together after he and his wife moved to Albany. In the meantime he had another idea for me. "You know this guy Gary Roemer? At UCLA? He's been doing some cool stuff with foxes in the Channel Islands. He's about to wrap up that study, so I'm not sure how much longer he'll be out there. But you should talk to him. If you could get a look at his stuff on the foxes, that would be a good way to get your feet wet." Which is exactly what happened.

2 ≋ The Island of Missing Foxes

A MONTH LATER I STEPPED OFF THE PACKET BOAT INTO THE shallows of Prisoners Harbor off Santa Cruz Island. Gary Roemer had been quick with an invitation. I contacted him not only because Roland recommended him but because I knew it was unlikely I could stay with either Elise's work on the Darwin's fox or Roland's yet-to-begin study of coyotes long enough to see their completions. Each of these projects would consume several years, and the trip to Santa Cruz was a chance to see the wind-up phase of a long-term study. Gary said he was crossing the Santa Barbara Channel fairly regularly to do follow-up research on his most recent finding: that on a number of the Channel Islands, the fox was in trouble.

Along with a graduate student in entomology named Frances Edillo, and a gaggle of fun-hog kayakers, we took the packet boat from Ventura. At the dockside ticket kiosk there was a postcard showing the Channel Island fox, the emblem of the islands. It showed a small gray fox with a tinge of russet on its legs. It stood on a dry, grassy hill, looking into the distance. Although they are small and so docile that Gary was able to handle them without sedation, the Island foxes had by default been the top predators on the Channel Islands ever since DDT wiped out the bald eagles. Now, on Santa Cruz Island, the foxes too were approaching extinction.

Gary was on his way to the island to investigate the possibility that heartworm, a common parasite of domestic dogs, was killing off the foxes. He was a much livelier person, physically stronger and more intense, than his flat midwestern accent had led me to expect from our phone conversations. He had brown eyes and an absolutely direct gaze that was inquisitive and maybe a little wary. His humor was at the ready, and he was dressed like the fun-hogs in shorts, T-shirt, and Tevas. But he was somehow too focused on the tasks at hand to be mistaken for one of them. He seemed to be able to carry all our considerable gear—clothes, four days' food, two picnic coolers full of dry ice, and a big carton packed with mosquito traps—at once, and he stowed it under the front deck of the packet with the kayaks. Frances and I settled on deck near the bow and the spray. She was a tiny Filipino woman, educated in Japan before coming to UCLA. She talked with abandon about her family, her experience of the United States, and the progress of her career. Since high school, she had focused doggedly on becoming a scientist, and although attaining status as a professional in her field was not far off, she was taking nothing for granted. Occasionally, Gary, who had spent twelve years crossing the Santa Barbara Channel, came up to the bow to interrupt our chatter with some observation about the channel currents or the silhouette of the island, which was growing more distinct on the horizon.

Santa Cruz, one of the northern cluster of California's Channel Islands, lies in a luxury of idyllic water across the channel from Ventura. The island has been a preserve for the last decade and is held by the Nature Conservancy and by the National Park Service, which owns about 24 percent of it. Santa Cruz is about twenty-three miles long and vaguely scorpion-shaped, which explains why our first stop was called Scorpion Anchorage. Seals and dolphins played in the cove. Marine mammals were what the kayakers came to see. They were not interested in the dry interiors of the mountains that rose up from the ocean to form much of the island's coast. The boat released the kayakers to a tall concrete pier here. Our boat followed the craggy face of the island for a couple of miles and then stopped fifty yards off shore. Prisoners Harbor was a low place with a short run of sand beach where a creek met the ocean. We loaded a raft with the coolers and other gear, and one of the packet boat crew took the oars.

The beach was deserted, but there was, mysteriously, a jeep waiting under a tree. Gary was familiar with the jeep. It belonged to the research station that the University of California maintains on the island. "They left us the old one," Gary observed, but he accepted this fate cheerfully, walking around the vehicle to inspect the tires. "Not too bad. Not much worse than last time." What remained of the treads were shadows of their patterns on the slick rubber. I paid no attention to this inspection because I had no idea of the places the jeep would carry us in the days ahead. Neither did Frances, because on a previous trip she had ridden all over Santa Cruz in the same jeep. Her only concern about the jeep was how to force all the coolers into the narrow boot in the back.

The mission of the next few days was hers. She was there to trap and identify mosquitoes and to determine whether any of them carried the egg of the heartworm. This was a career matter and very important. Her neat trousers and camp shirt had been carefully selected for the heat on the island and the work ahead, and as soon as we packed into the jeep with Gary, she left off the chat and limited her comments to science. She had explained to me during the channel crossing that it was important that he, her partner in the research, regard her as a professional.

Gary's T-shirt had a hole at the back of the neck, and he was oblivious to the abrupt alteration in Frances. He had his degrees, his driver's license for science, and although nothing about his current position as a postdoc was secure, he was living his role as a scientist without self-consciousness. He was in high spirits as he drove up the road that led into the island. His knowledge of the place was intimate, and he wanted to be sure that Frances and I did not miss any salient detail. His commentary was punctuated by a dry, cackly laugh and the grinding of metal every time the jeep slipped out of gear. The gravel road faded into a dry, rocky creek bed, a transition Gary didn't seem to notice, and the jeep bucked merrily between two ragged rock faces. Frances endured the jounces and Gary's commentary politely. The temperature rose with our distance from the water.

"Bet that's a good place to get some mosquitoes." He stopped the jeep and pointed to a cove in the rock where the mesquite was thick and made a dark shade. To me he said, "We might see a fox or two while you're here." It had never occurred to me that we wouldn't see the foxes. Even though I knew they were in danger, I didn't yet understand the extent of the damage to the Santa Cruz population.

It was possible that mosquitoes were the connection to the crash of the fox population. When Gary had arrived on Santa Cruz as a master's degree student to help out with the fox research, the foxes were numerous and unworried about being seen. After five years of fox work, he began a two-year research project of his own. He lived in a dilapidated trailer on the wind-blasted west end of Santa Cruz and spent his days trapping and tracking foxes. He had good success trapping using a very systematic grid layout. The foxes were quite unafraid, and he was able to collar them and take samples without tranquilizing them—he also dealt barehanded with the spotted skunks he sometimes caught in the fox traps. He was able to recapture many of the foxes he had collared and to monitor their health. He spent the next four years coming back and forth across the Santa Barbara Channel. He had plenty of fox data. "I like this kind of long-term study," he told me and mentioned the work of David Mech on wolves and George Schaller on lions. He thought there was value and depth in watching the animals over time—especially in terms of their conservation. I noticed that, for Gary, conservation was inextricable from biology.

He didn't seem to mind the time he had given to the Santa Cruz foxes. His first years on the island produced a dissertation that was essentially a set of answers to the question, What is this animal doing here? It was a natural history of the Island fox: what it eats, how much territory it requires and how it travels, if and how it is related to other foxes nearby, and how it shares territory with these and other mammals on the island. He wrote a full description of the animal and what it was doing in that place. It was a good thing he had documented all this because a year or so after submitting his dissertation, while he was casting about for a new research project, he visited the island. He found the foxes were almost gone. He was baffled and alarmed, but because he had already established the essential facts of the Island fox's life, he was uniquely positioned to figure out why the Santa Cruz population was going off the rails. With so much already invested in the Island fox, he could hardly afford not to try to figure out what was going on. He reenlisted.

During his second round of fox study, Gary stepped back from the particulars of the foxes' foraging, territory, and reproduction to look at the island's animal systems, the network of eat-and-be-eaten. This is a standard ecological approach with a long history. What does this animal eat? was a topic about which Darwin speculated routinely as he ventured out from the *Beagle* to see what unfamiliar species would present itself. So simple on its face. But it led deeper down a far more complicated path than I had expected. I was well aware that food, what the animals ate, would be a topic of concern in all the field research I would visit. I had written plenty of radio shorts pointing out that this bird or that snake "needed" a particular kind of food, and along the way, a number of biologists had told me that the question of what an animal eats is the most important question to ask about it. Certainly I understood that need was the margin between success and desperation. But I did not appreciate, and certainly not at the depth I do now, how food controls what an animal does and is.

What Darwin was really asking was, What does this animal eat that keeps it alive in this place? Current thinking expands this question to include the notions of work and energy. What an animal eats determines how far it has to travel to find that food. And vice versa. How far an animal travels equals what it needs to eat.

The hypothesis Gary developed about the domino-like chain of predation attempted to account for the effects of game pieces that had been taken out of play: bald eagles, the original top predators on the island, had been eliminated from it by DDT. For years, this left the foxes at the top of the sparsely populated system on Santa Cruz—*depauperate* was the word Gary used by way of introduction. Not many species of animals or plants. Golden eagles had recently begun nesting on the island, and the big draw for the golden eagles was the piglets of the feral hogs that rooted all over the island. The foxes, unaccustomed to being victims of predators, often allowed themselves to be caught in the open, and they were snatched and killed along with the succulent pigs.

Gary's balancing of the eagle's energy intake and effort output had its origins in ideas about the energy economics of animal life that emerged from research done in the late 1960s and 1970s on birds. Applying these ideas to carnivores, David Macdonald, among others, devised a more complex scheme to explain the broad variations in the animals' territory holding, sociality, and breeding arrangements. The Resource Dispersion Hypothesis was first proposed more than twenty years ago and is now referred to fondly in the literature as the "RDH." Looking at how food is concentrated over space and time, the RDH uses the notion of "patchy" food availability to relate the body size of a predator to the body size of prey and then to territory size, number of offspring and how they are cared for, and the degree of their sociality.

What the RDH boils down to is that if there is food enough in one place for more than one animal at the same time, that animal is more likely to live in social groups. If the calories are spread out over space or time, these are more likely to be pursued by solitary animals. Because they are so flexible in their living arrangements, animals in the dog family, the canids, offer convenient demonstrations of the RDH. At one extreme are the African hunting dogs. They live in tensely organized packs formed around a single breeding female, and the packs hunt together over territories of more than five hundred square miles. Their coordinated attacks allow the packs to take down much larger prey animals, sometimes as large as a zebra, than an individual wild dog would be capable of killing. The calories that result are shared all around and are brought back to the den in regurgitated form if there is a litter with pup-sitters. How far you travel equals what you need to eat: Big territory, many eaters, big kill.

At the other extreme is a canid like the Island fox, a small, solitary traveler who forages in a small circumscribed territory, has not been routinely exposed to danger, and doesn't have to compete for the food. What you need to eat equals how far you travel: Small territory, and a mouse is a real prize.

While none of these dogs with their various living arrangements is assured of a happy balancing of the time-distance-calorie equation, in terms of durability of their species, foxes in general have an edge over the dedicated carnivory of the African hunting dog. A picky eater is a vulnerable animal, John Gittleman pointed out to me. "If you are an animal, the best way for you to go extinct is to eat only meat."

But the crash of the Island fox population on Santa Cruz Island was not the result of a lack of food. Until some other explanation prevails, it was the result of an abundance of food, the feral piglets. Until they drew the golden eagles to the island, the small fox had been lord in the island's short food chain, sharing only some of its food with the spotted skunk, which would also become an incidental victim of the eagle's hunting. Over a period of seventeen months, Gary Roemer and his team found twenty-one dead foxes on the island. All the carcasses showed evidence of eagle attack—talon holes in the pelt and "de-gloved" forelegs and paws from which the skin had been peeled. There were feathers near some of the carcasses, and they found an eagle's nest containing the remains of fox and skunk. The most impressive evidence, though, was the fact that some of the eagles later removed from the island smelled like skunk. Still, a court of biologists might have considered all this circumstantial evidence of the cause of the population crash. So, as a precautionary measure to eliminate disease—which can be especially devastating to a marooned island population—as a possible cause of the crash, Gary sent the carcasses to the veterinary school at UC Davis for tests. These turned up nothing.

Tightening his case against the golden eagles, Gary created a mathematical model to answer the question, Could the golden eagles on their own have brought about the devastation of the foxes? The simulated answer was, "Easily." Now implicating the feral hogs, Gary asked, Are the foxes and skunks themselves good enough food to lure the eagles twenty-five miles over the ocean? He answered this with a series of calculations involving the caloric values of fox and skunk carcasses and the time-distance-energy budget for an eagle that must fly across the Santa Barbara Channel. No surprise, the scrawny foxes didn't make enough of a meal to justify the flight to Santa Cruz. But once the eagles were hovering over the island looking for piglets, it was just as convenient to kill an unwary fox or skunk caught in the open as it was to nail a piglet. Somehow the package deal not only satisfied the needs of a single eagle but provided enough calories to allow the new top predator to invite company and share the bounty.

Gary had begun publishing articles substantiating this theory when it was suggested that heartworm, the same parasite that infests and kills pet dogs, might be another contributing cause of the foxes' disappearance. The eggs that produce the larvae that congregate in the chambers of the host dog's heart are carried by several species of mosquitoes.

He was skeptical about this possibility. But there was money available to fund an investigation, and he thought it was worth a shot. At the very least, it provided a means for him to continue his work on the island for a short time. When I asked about the cooler full of dry ice behind the seat, he said, "Think about it. What is it about you that draws mosquitoes? Carbon dioxide. All mammals, all good sources of blood, give off carbon dioxide." There were plenty of prospective customers for Frances's traps, and there were a number of moments in our travels around the island when the air was filled with mosquitoes and I resolved to stop exhaling.

The creek bed that was our road approached the central valley of the island, and as soon as we were out of sight of the ocean, I began to notice the smell of licorice. "Fennel," Gary announced. This part of the island had been cultivated by successive waves of optimists—Russian whalers, Italians, and Chinese—and most recently it had been home to a cattle ranch. The Italians had planted the fennel, and they had also introduced hogs that became feral and were now rampant on the island. The isolation of Santa Cruz and the other Channel Islands by the Pacific, which had protected the emergence of the Channel Island fox as a species, also made the islands vulnerable to unhealthy blooms of imported species like the hogs and the fennel. Santa Cruz had no plants aggressive enough to compete with the stout fennel and no indigenous predators large enough to take down a hog. Its sea cliffs were a rock-bound garden wall.

The jeep came out into a meadow of long, dry grass, where there was a house, a barn, and some sheds. This was headquarters for the Nature Conservancy, and a dirt road connected it to the low, red building that housed the University of California field station, which had been in operation since before the island's conversion to a preserve. Farther out the road were the three cabins that served as a camp kitchen and two bunk rooms, also owned by the Nature Conservancy. We stowed the food—Frances's frozen dinners and Gary's healthy stuff—and moved into the bunk cabins. In the early afternoon, Gary arrived at the door of the cabin I shared with Frances to announce with some satisfaction that the copperhead that had been nesting under his cabin was still there, coming and going as usual. We walked out into the central valley, a long cleft between the two ridges of small mountains that ran east-west to almost touch both ends of the island. The sides of the mountains were smooth and covered with palomino grasses. It was May, but the sky was pale, and the heat became intense. The mountains, grasses, the creek beds, and drainages were dry, surprisingly dry for spring.

In this season, Santa Cruz Island was an arid rock standing in the Pacific, sheltered by the ocean from the clamor and buffeting of people and their projects. Gary took us to a place where, amazingly, there was water. A spring-fed creek poured over the rock into a well it had carved in its stone run. He took off his shirt, dove in, and churned around for a while. He teased Frances and me about not swimming, and I envied his easy access to the cool water. But we were a fair dis-

tance from the cabins, and the prospect of walking in the heat with a
tangle of wet underwear kept me from wading in past my knees. He
didn't care. He was having fun. After a few minutes he paused and
treaded the cool water to answer my questions about how he had
come to Santa Cruz in the first place, why he had been so long on the
island, and what kept him there.

He was older, he thought, than the usual postdoc at the brink of
a scientific career. He came from Wisconsin, where his father worked
in a factory and lived for vacations when he could take his sons camping and hunting. Gary was in college at Parkside when an anatomy
professor ignited his interest in biology. After that it took a long time
to get to the work for his master's degree. He started this under Robert
Wayne, who was at the time just establishing himself as an authority
on canid genetics and on genetic techniques for determining identity
and relatedness. Wayne had started some basic research on Channel
Island foxes, and Gary began the detail work for this. He worked on
the island for five years before moving past the master's requirements
and continuing the research for his doctorate. Often he had difficulties with money. But his time on the island forged a strong attachment
to it and a commitment to *Urocyon littoralis,* the Island fox. Sometimes it was still a battle.

"I'm outspoken," he said. "Maybe I'm too outspoken. For instance,
I don't think the state is spending enough to help the foxes, and I've
managed to make some people mad." He came up dripping from the
pool and strapped his sandals back on his feet. "And," his honesty was
as disarming as his forthright gaze, "I have a temper. Frances knows
that, don't you, Frances?"

Frances escaped comment with a little smile. I had no idea what
had transpired, but whatever had gone on was not scaring her off.

In the early evening, we put the box of mosquito traps and the
cooler filled with dry ice in the back of the jeep and set out in the
creek bed for a place Gary called Hanging Valley. The island's copper
soil was easily visible under the dry grasses, the mesquite, and the
scrub. "Depauperate," Gary said again about the biology of the stony
desert contained by the cliffs and the ocean. He liked Latinate words
and Latin species names.

The creek bed merged with a track that lined the edges of the steep
hills and the grayer, somewhat greener valleys. In the steep places, the

track was barely wide enough for the jeep, which ground through the switchbacks, skipping through the gears with the grating of metal parts. I watched chunks of copper-colored earth break away from the ragged edge of the mountain and drop into high space. Gary was oblivious to the steepness and the tight curves, and if we happened to be rounding a sheer place and he happened to see something that interested him—a grass or flower, fox scat or skunk sign—he would stop the jeep on the edge of the curve and get out to take a closer look. "Look at this!" He would pluck a sprig of whatever it was and announce its Latin name. He was intent on pointing out the details of the island's biology. "Eh-henh! Something wrong with this little fox. See this diarrhea?" But even after twelve years on the island he was still finding pieces of its natural system that he didn't recognize. If he couldn't come up with the name, he would tuck the leaf or flower into the army-issue canvas pouch that carried his field notebook and pen.

In the notebook he recorded every observation that related to the foxes, the skunks, or the island's bird life. He showed me his notes of our visit thus far. They were beautiful in their order. He kept his observations according to a strict system he had learned from a professor who had done graduate work at Berkeley, where the system originated and was strictly preserved. "Do you know that there is a room at Berkeley where they store the field notes of all these people who did graduate work there?" The method suited him well. He was a very systematic thinker. For my work in radio I had interviewed scores of scientists, but it was Gary who impressed on me one of the big differences in the way scientists think and the way I think. I had been educated to be aware of ideas and ways of thinking. Gary had been trained to think inductively, to drill down to fact.

Now the island's mosquitoes were very much subjects of his methodical inquiry. Each of the mosquito traps stowed in the back of the jeep was a plastic cylinder, inside of which was mounted a small, battery-driven fan. Attached to one end of the cylinder was a fine mesh bag. We hung the traps in trees, usually in darker places where the air was still. Under the net bag we hung a plastic bucket that held a chunk of dry ice wrapped in newspaper. The mosquitoes would hover over the dry ice vapors rising from the cylinder, and the fan would suck them down into the mesh bag, where they would lie until Frances could count and classify them.

Each day progressed in the same sequence. In the morning we emptied the traps into plastic jars marked with the trap location and the date. Frances had plenty of specimens to examine, and now, like Gary, she was recording things in a notebook. In the evening we replenished the dry ice and maybe repositioned some traps, and then we returned to the kitchen building, where Gary set up a Coleman lamp and Frances brought out a microscope and an enormous manual detailing the astonishing number of mosquito species in California.

This was the one period during the day when we weren't moving around and when there was time for conversation. I enjoyed talking with Gary because he takes ideas quite seriously, and he's feisty. One night he said that reading Darwin had caused him to slough off his religious upbringing. The ideas embodied in each seemed mutually exclusive, and since Darwin was the greatest modern thinker, religion had to go. Darwin himself was troubled by the fact that his theory of evolution threatened conventional convictions about divine creation, and after coming under attack by leading churchmen and a number of prominent scientists, he softened somewhat his statements of his theory. When I mentioned a new book that examined the ideas of Freud and Darwin and their influence, Gary said, "In the same book? Don't you think that's crazy?"

"No."

"You should think about that, Holly. I mean Darwin and *Freud*? They're not even comparable." One was a giant, the other a dwarf.

I didn't say that I hadn't actually read Darwin's work yet because Gary might have found that lapse intolerable, and when I did begin reading, I found that Darwin had been trained—in medical school and by the example of his older gentrified colleagues—to think in a mode like Gary's. He too loved fact. He too had had been taught how to take notes by another scientist.

I learned that Darwin's response to almost every natural occurrence was strangely like my own upon coming face-to-face with the coyote in the hayfield: What is this—this rock, this plant, this animal—doing here? His journal recorded the presence of a tumult of boulders or the shoals at the mouth of a river with speculations about the rising and falling of the ocean and the upheaval from below the surface of the earth. His researches on the fauna he encountered ran parallel. He tried to determine what linked the animal to its place, especially food, and speculated on its enemies, including its attitude toward humans. He tried to imagine how it managed to survive.

Darwin knew that his questions were the most basic ones, that any answers he suggested would branch into more specific questions, and that the answers to these would split into further inquiries. He knew how science worked. From his years at Cambridge and his informal associations with others pursuing natural history, Darwin was thoroughly conversant with scientific literature, accounts of earlier voyages, and current conventions of discovery. They were about collecting and naming. Like his colleagues, he recognized the vastness of the natural world and the daunting variety of what he called its "productions." Although he occasionally revealed an awareness of the vulnerability of a plant or animal population, he was, for the most part, too much in the hold of the multitude, variety, and beginnings of nature's productions to ponder their disintegration or downright destruction.

Unlike his hero, however, Gary was now preoccupied by the dwindling of a species and the mysteries of its disappearance. He may have harbored doubts about the heartworm explanation, but he explored it with habitual intensity. All the time he was talking, Gary's attention was on the microscope and the manual. He moved in and out of the aura of the gas lamp to peer into the microscope and make his own conclusions about exactly which of the confusingly similar species was prone on the glass slide at the moment. Frances endured this patiently for an hour or so and then closed the manual and announced that the identification of the rest of the tiny black corpses would have to wait for daylight. Gary would have stayed up all night to work through the pile of dead mosquitoes, but Frances closing the identification manual became a part of the routine.

We careered around the red dirt roads for three more days, harvesting mosquitoes out of the net sleeves and setting out dry ice. Occasionally a small, dark hog burst from the underbrush to scramble across the road. The island's feral hogs were small, about the size of a pig-roast candidate, with dark bristles and darker spots underneath. Their tails curled up like the ones on piglets in a picture book. Even though the Nature Conservancy had supplied a rifle with which to dispatch the hogs, Gary had been ignoring them. I wondered about this because he had grown up with rifles and clearly knew how to knock off the invaders. Did my presence make him self-conscious? Or

perhaps, because he wasn't trying to account for the hogs systematically, they weren't worth the distraction of unpacking the gun. I didn't
ask him about this right away.

Evidently the golden eagles wouldn't be granted the same leniency.
I was the one to spot the bird, and the jeep slammed to a halt. Gary
brought up his binoculars. The bird, whatever it was, was soaring very
high, and against the hot, hazy sky it appeared smaller than I would
have expected an eagle to be. But Gary said, "Yup. That's what it is.
Golden eagle. Good spotting—now we'll have to find out where it's
nesting." He would try to catch the bird with a net trap, crate it up,
and take it off the island to a release site where there was enough good
hunting to make it forget Santa Cruz Island. He had already removed
a number of eagles and hoped this one wasn't a recidivist back for
another go at the Island foxes.

A good deal of money has gone into zoological research on the
Channel Islands, some of which Gary helped raise. The sums are large
enough to make the other field biologists I traveled with blush at their
meager budgets. The funds are not large enough, however, to do what
Gary thinks needs to be done. Given the expectations that he and the
rest of Californians have for the islands, he is probably right. Moving
eagles around and culling wild hogs are only part of it. On Santa
Catalina in the southern group of islands, where, because of the resort
on the island, not all of it is incorporated into the national park,
about 90 percent of the Island foxes have been wiped out by distemper, and rodents overrun the beaches. On San Miguel and Santa Rosa
islands, where there are both a captive-breeding program and concern
about the viability of the loggerhead shrike, the foxes are rounded up
every year before the loggerheads begin to nest, and they are detained
until the nestlings fledge and are safely on the wing. The effects of
these projects have to be monitored by ongoing research, no small expense in itself.

Any number of other people who lived or who had lived on the
island and were back seemed to share Gary's sense of belonging to
Santa Cruz and being responsible for it, a kind of ownership. If the
propaganda in the Park Service dockside concession was any indication, Californians at large were engaged in the well-being of nature on
all the Channel Islands.

At the UC Research Station, we came across Jeff Howarth and his girlfriend. Jeff was a graduate student in geography who had previously worked as Gary's field assistant. Now he was engaged in an effort to create a historical map of the island using GPS readings to reconcile all the maps made by people in all the earlier waves of settlement. Howarth's map would take into account not only buildings and roads and piers but the layout of streams and plants from the time Native Americans lived on the island. He would look past the rank fennel and the plants it had squeezed out to much earlier successions before people had begun to impose their notions of what kinds of plants—grapes, hay—might better grow there. Gary took the same keen interest in the progress of the map that he takes about anything to do with Santa Cruz, and I wondered if it was in the back of his mind that the island should be replanted to reflect Howarth's findings. The elaborateness of conservation efforts in the islands made me wonder if the map Jeff Howarth eventually drew wouldn't be viewed as a kind of blueprint for returning Santa Cruz to its original natural state, a set of specifications for Eden, where death—death of a species—is impossible.

If returning the island to its original natural state was the goal, I decided, the jeep and the other gas-powered vehicles should go.

"Know what I'm getting you for Christmas, Gary?"

The notion that I would think of him at Christmas caught him off guard. "What?" he said cautiously.

"A mule."

"A *mule?*"

"What you need out here is a mule—it could take you all the places you can't go in this jeep. Be a lot safer than this jeep."

"This jeep's okay."

"Less polluting . . . more fun . . ."

"Send two," he cackled, seeing the ultimate advantage of this sterile hybrid equine. "No danger of their overrunning the island like these hogs."

On a side trip we went as far as the Christi Ranch, where the western edge of the island meets the Pacific. The airstrip and the house and the barns, preserved for occasional retreats, lie in a wide, grassy swale where a creek runs to the ocean. It is a bright, serene place not too far from the point where Gary lived and trapped while he was doing his dissertation research. He indicated the slopes where his traps had been. There was very little cover, and I wondered that a fox would live in such open country, but he assured me that he had found them there in healthy numbers. Using one hand to drive and the other to trace a diagram, he mapped out the grid pattern he used to locate his traps. He set cage traps in a grid, put ear tags on the foxes he caught, and then a year later used the same trap layout to recapture the tagged foxes and compare the location of the traps and the foxes' sizes, health, and reproductive status with those facts from a year earlier. The animals did not need to be sedated to be collared and handled during the physical examination and blood-taking, and the experience of being trapped and handled didn't bother them enough to prevent them from walking into another trap the next season. The scheme and the results, I realized after I had seen more field research, were as close to ideal as he could get.

As Darwin and his early coauthor on evolution, Alfred Russel Wallace, found long before Gary took advantage of it, an island is a convenient place to study any of nature's productions. An island's plants and animals are captives of the ocean, and this, as Darwin and Wallace sensed but did not articulate, makes the island an evolutionary pressure cooker. The foxes on Santa Cruz had nowhere else to go, and they turned up over and over in his traps. The grid, Gary said, provided consistency to the data on the foxes that he caught and recaught on the slope. Trap location and fox identity, as established by ear tags, were two absolute values for a group of highly variable subjects.

He began to give me a description of his genetic detective work to determine the structure of the island's fox families. "Well, it starts with PCR of course because that's the replication process that made this kind of analysis possible. So let's start there. You know about PCR?"

PCR. PCR? All I could think of was PRC, People's Republic of China.

"Polymerase chain reaction. Basic. It's something you should know. Look it up when you get home—it's in any introductory genetics text."

Start with the first fact, move on to the next. Systematization bolstered the validity of fact, about which he was a stickler, and so he didn't finish telling me about his genetic assays. If I wanted to find out the results of his DNA work, I would have to look up PCR. Which I did. After I returned home, I found a basic description of the chemical process that replicates a small amount of DNA until there is enough of the stuff to analyze.

Gary seemed confident of the fact that there were still a few foxes and the fact that some were cubs. I wanted to see a fox because I believed that in order to understand the Island fox, I would have to actually lay eyes on it. I watched the bushes and boulders along the road, hoping to catch a glimpse of a sharp muzzle and bright eyes.

"They're out during the day," Gary assured me about the foxes, "because they haven't had any predators to hide from until now. That's probably one reason the eagles get them."

The Island fox had learned not to be on guard or secretive. At its previously high numbers, random happenstance would have caused one of them to appear in the track ahead of the jeep. But that didn't happen. We saw the scat, but not the animals themselves. Gary didn't seem concerned about our lack of sightings per se but about the fact that there were too few foxes for the law of averages to bring one of them into our presence.

He kept saying, "We'll probably see the fox that hangs out by the field station," because he would have liked to show me a fox the way he had shown me so many of the island's other natural features.

I watched closely every time the jeep emerged from the grove of eucalyptus near the field station. Nothing stirred in its vicinity.

The idyll ended. Gary drove Frances and me and the mosquito specimens out to Prisoners Harbor to meet the boat. My time on the island was over, I hadn't gotten up the nerve to ask Gary about the rifle and the feral hogs. I find it difficult to ask honest questions when I have already formed a strong opinion, and at the time my opinion was that trying to restore the island to its original state would be hubris. No one could possibly have or gain enough detailed information to do this. Gary taxied Frances and me out the dry creek bed toward Prisoners Harbor. Another black-haired hog crashed out of the mesquite not far from the farmstead. The rifle stayed put in its case.

"You haven't shot any hogs on this trip," I observed.

"Nope."

"Would you have shot any of them if I hadn't been along?"

"No, it wasn't that I—" He thought better of whatever he would have said. But evidently he too had something he had been wanting to ask, because after a good half hour of the jeep bumping along the creek bed, he said, "Holly, are you one of those animal rights people?"

I laughed. "No, what I was trying to get around to was all this tinkering . . ."

"*Tinkering?*" He had no idea what I was referring to.

"Moving eagles around, killing off hogs, corralling foxes so the shrikes can fledge. I mean, trying to restore the island to whatever you and the rest of them think its original state might have been."

He was not offended, and he did not stop shifting gears. "I think what I'm doing—what we're doing—here is right, if that's what you're asking."

"Would you go so far as to replant the island or part of it to make it good-as-new?"

"Well," he cackled, "it would be nice to get rid of this fennel, wouldn't it?"

"But who decides what the original was? Who decides what the balance should be, what the ideal is?"

"That's a tough call." He was taking me seriously, and he had rolled all of this around in his head before. "Those decisions have to be the very best estimates made with the best information we have—which is never perfect."

"Why do you have to do anything at all?"

"Because," he explained as patiently as a first-grade teacher, "these foxes can very well go *extinct*." The prospect made him genuinely anxious, and his response made a strong impression on me for what it implied about the difference between humans and animals living wild. Humans have the power to imagine the future, and our ability to look ahead is the basis of conservation. As strong a defender of animal intellect as I am, I doubt that a fox has this capacity.

At the beach the boat idled in the shallows. Workers were offloading rolls of fencing, and Gary gave us an unhappy account of this. When the Nature Conservancy had become overburdened by the costs of maintaining all of its holdings on Santa Cruz Island, the organization had turned over part of its land to the National Park Service. Now the Conservancy was fencing off its area of the island to increase the efficiency of its hog-eradication program. The fence would be both hog-proof and fox-proof. It would create two islands, he explained, a gloomy prospect. But there was, so far as he could see, nothing to be done about it. Gary waited with us while the launch crossed back and forth over the shallows with fencing, posts, and tools. He was staying a few more days on Santa Cruz.

"Sorry you didn't get to see a fox," he said.

"That's the point, isn't it?" I said about the population crash, the foxes' sudden disappearance from the island.

"Yeah, but I know you would have liked to see one."

Quite true. But I assumed I would have other opportunities to see *Urocyon littoralis,* and just getting out to the island seemed important. The island had sheltered its fox the way the Galápagos had sheltered Darwin's finches, and they had lived there in strong numbers. But now the same island was conveniently corralling the foxes for roundup by a new top predator, and there were only a few left. Next to none. It was a place witnessing an extinction.

The Island foxes' fate had shifted rapidly because confinement makes everything that lives on an island more vulnerable to outside forces. It took Gary almost a decade to learn what the fox was doing on the island. Then, in a series of events set off initially by DDT, the Island fox was nearly wiped out in only three years. The fox had no escape route.

Islands are dangerous places. Santa Cruz was a naturally occurring island, and I would go from Gary's research there to research taking place on landlocked islands, patches of land isolated by human activity and yet through some means protected from it. The wild canids in all these places were similarly vulnerable.

Gary and I talked about my returning to Santa Cruz and maybe visiting other Channel Islands after I returned from Chile. Neither of us knew that Gary himself would leave California within a few months—he would take a teaching job at New Mexico State University, Las Cruces, and his outspoken advocacy for the foxes would cause friction with funders and other members of his research team and put more than geographical distance between him and the ongoing research on the Island fox. So I told him I would come back, and I promised myself it would be sometime when mosquito trapping didn't make travel by jeep necessary. I could walk up into the hills and through the drainages. Maybe on foot I would see one of the remaining foxes.

3 ≋ How to Set a Trap

WHILE IT WAS NOT NECESSARY FOR GARY TO ACTUALLY WIT-
ness the comings and goings of the foxes to learn something about
their requirements for territory and habitat, it was necessary for him
to trap and collar them. To answer many of the questions about an
animal's natural history, to get the information that puts or keeps the
animal under the protective wing of conservation, it is usually necessary to physically arrest it, however briefly. Darwin and his fellow
nineteenth-century collectors usually had to resort to permanently arresting their research subjects with guns. Now most of our information about wildlife hinges on the snapping of a trap. Leg-hold traps,
snares, cage traps, pitfalls set for larger animals, box and snap traps for
animals as small as rodents. Direct sedation delivered by dart is used
for the largest animals, particularly those inclined to panic at physical
confinement and hurt themselves, and researchers working on a number of different big cats have found that using hounds to run down
and corner a cat in order to dart it is less stressful for the cat than trying to hold it in a trap.

None of these devices makes trapping quick or sure-fire. Todd
Fuller, Elise's advisor at the University of Massachusetts, has directed
field research on carnivores all over the world, and I asked him how
technological advances—radios, GPS, DNA assays—had changed
work in the field over the course of his career. "Not much," he said.
"Not as much as you might think, because you still have to catch wild
animals, and it's just not that easy." He advised Elise to recruit Eric
York, an experienced trapper, for her research on the Darwin's fox. "I
didn't see why I would need Eric," she told me. "Now I don't see how
I could get along without him." Somehow Gary had made trapping
seem much easier. His grid system for capture-recapture implied it

could even be routine. But then, he had been trapping the same animals on the same islands for more than a decade.

When I began to work with Roland Kays, he was just starting up in new territory. Observing his work in the Pine Bush over a couple of years, I could see the truth in what Fuller was saying. Trapping is a finicky, potentially lethal, and always time-consuming art, and watching Roland proceed caused me to think harder about the things that scientists must do to animals to get information about them and how long it takes to accomplish them.

John Gittleman had sent me to Roland, saying, "You could have some fun with this." But on first meeting him in his new office at the New York State Museum, Roland Kays did not strike me as fun. Slight and wiry with short red-chestnut hair, small gold-rimmed glasses, and a gold earring, Roland presented himself quite soberly. He showed me pictures of himself in climbing harness working his way up a three-story tree in Panama and another holding a sedated kinkajou. He had slides of the parts of the animal, glands, paws, a carnassial tooth with a vertical groove in it. We talked about going to Panama to see the kinkajous and maybe doing an article. He was helpful, factual, just as he had been on the phone. So I accepted his seriousness at face value. This proved to be a mistake. I was merely getting his museum docent treatment, his way of dealing with the foolishness of nonscientists.

Roland said he'd be happy to have me visit the coyote research, but he seemed wary. He probably couldn't figure out what I wanted, and I, wary of how young he was for the position he held and of his instant, confident answers to my questions, took him at first as a climber of more than trees. Another misjudgment. The gold earring should have tipped me off. While Roland can put a serious face on science—because he is, in fact, serious about science—behind that is a playfulness. It is a playfulness that has to do with the possibilities of fact.

I arranged to meet him at a shiny silver diner on Route 20, which runs along the southern boundary of the Pine Bush Preserve. I got mildly lost on the tangle of interstates around Albany, and when I found the diner Roland had finished his coffee, a bagel, and a journal article on coyotes in the West. He was eager to be off.

"We should take my truck," he said. "I hope you don't mind. There are some dead coyotes in back—but they're frozen."

He wanted to check the condition of the dead coyotes before we started out. They were not Pine Bush coyotes. They were the gift of a trapper who worked near the town of Paul Smiths in the Adirondacks. Under the truck cap there were a couple of heavy cardboard boxes. I am afraid of dead things. I am not squeamish at the sight of trauma or blood. But I dread the item in which the blood has stopped circulating. I hoped this wasn't evident.

Under the lid of the first carton was the body of a coyote in a clear plastic bag. Then bags of ice, the kind you buy for a party, another carcass in a plastic bag, and so on. The coyote on top had the wide, dull eyes of the dead, and its tongue flopped out of its open jaw. The fur was dense and surprisingly long, and it was not the simple brindle gray I had seen at a distance. Under the topcoat there were patches that glowed chestnut and gold. The carcasses were intended eventually for Matt Gompper, a scientist then at Columbia University and a friend of Roland's. He was studying the coyotes near New York City and wanted to do some genetic comparisons with animals in the northern part of the state.

"They'll keep for a while," Roland decided about the carcasses. "We can hike first, then deal with these guys."

The Pine Bush Preserve is a patchwork of discontinuous tracts of pine barrens that account for 2,940 acres on both sides of the New York State Thruway. It exists in what was the bottom of a glacial lake, and on its shallow, sandy hills are stands of rare pitch pine and oak. The first land was purchased for the preserve in 1974, too late to erase the roads and housing and office buildings that had been springing up since the 1920s. It seems remarkable that the little plots of sand and trees dotting the suburb like so many little islands function as a preserve. But the Pine Bush does provide space and protection for a number of endangered plants and insects, including the rare Karner blue butterfly, which gave impetus to the creation of the preserve.

The coyotes in the Pine Bush are the so-called eastern coyote, the same species as the coyotes that live west of the Mississippi River, the one depicted in the Southwest with its head thrown back singing to a crescent moon, *Canis latrans.* Eastern coyotes are larger than those in the West, six to nine pounds heavier, and a number of trappers have reported finding it a challenge to distinguish the eastern coyote from the eastern gray wolf, which is smaller than the wolves in the West. The appearance, or the reappearance, of the coyote east of the Mississippi is relatively recent. Lewis and Clark had to travel as far west as Nebraska before they saw their first "prairie wolf." The most common explanation for the coyote's presence in the East today is that, beginning in the late nineteenth century, trapping and hunting wiped out the gray wolf and red wolf in the East, and coyotes began to move north and east to work those territories left vacant by the wolves. When one top dog moves out, another dog moves in and takes control. A second, emerging explanation is that coyotes have always lived in the East, that they too were devastated by hunting, trapping, and disease, and that the remnant animals are making a comeback unhampered by the presence of another top dog.

If prey calories are more, territories may be smaller. But if need be, coyotes can range as far as fifty miles in their hunting. If prey animals are large enough and numerous enough, coyotes may "pack up," as Roland calls it, and hunt cooperatively. While coyotes do not have the intense sociality of wolves, which usually hunt cooperatively and arrange breeding and pup rearing on the basis of pack hierarchy, it is not unusual for coyotes to raise young cooperatively. Recent work relates both packing up and population growth to "persecution." Roland uses this term frequently and with scientific blandness, devoid of judgment of the persecutors. If a male coyote is killed, that leaves his territory open, and another male that might otherwise be a nonbreeding member of another pack moves in to hold down the real estate and to breed a female.

One motive for persecuting coyotes is undoubtedly its reputation. While the fox has been typed as clever and quick-witted, and something of a gamesman rollicking through the human realm, the coyote is more of a low-life con operating beyond human reach—in fact, in Mexico, *coyote* refers to a shyster who knows how to cut through red tape. Long before Europeans encountered the coyote, Native Americans in any number of tribes had already given him leading roles in their myths. Almost always male, he was a liar, a lecher, a cheat, a silver tongue capable of talking his way out of even the tightest scrape, but also an embodiment of strength and resilience. In one legend from British Columbia, lowly Coyote is looking for a wife, and he outsmarts and disarms a beautiful young woman notorious for killing young men as she made love to them. Coyote marries her, thwarts the various murder plots of her father, arranges the old man's death by killer whale, and then, when his now much tamer wife produces a son, runs off with the baby. In another tale comparing the intelligence of Coyote and the white man, a storekeeper demands a demonstration of Coyote's trickery. He is bamboozled right on the spot. Coyote rides out of town on the shopkeeper's horse, wearing his clothes and leaving the white man bare-assed. Later the cowboys propagated their own myths of coyote cunning, some of which edge so close to nature that the stories could almost be true. These are the source of an apparently common belief that coyotes suffering attempts to kill them by trapping or shooting were smart enough to play dead until they saw an opportunity to escape.

In the mid-1970s, before the Pine Bush Preserve was established, coyotes had not yet been noticed, and it is not clear exactly when they moved in. But farther south, in the Finger Lakes, they've been seen for only the past ten years or so, and still farther south along the Hudson River near New York City, where Matt Gompper was observing them, more recently than that. This migration to the suburbs calls the question, Why is this big, wide-ranging carnivore sticking so close to where people live?

A couple of miles from the diner, we turned a corner, and Roland pulled up beside a tract of land where there was an office building going up. It was a couple of raw, rude acres where hillocks of ochre-colored earth proceeded toward the foundation of the building alongside a drive that had been plowed into the site. Roland took a camera from his backpack, got out of the truck, strode quickly out on the torn-up dirt, and lifted the camera.

"Good demonstration," he said about the photos he took there. Of the land-fracturing forces working against the Pine Bush, I assumed.

We went to a sandy trailhead just off a cul-de-sac in a middle-class development. Roland started off at a strong walk, still getting into his backpack. He likes to go first and to go fast. He enjoys the physicality of his work and seemed to look forward to what a walk might turn up. The weather was mild for November and characteristically cloudy but bright. We were looking for scat, primarily coyote scat but also the feces of other animals that might be food or competition for the coyotes. Roland and his assistant had been walking these trails on a regular schedule, collecting any new droppings that had been deposited and noting the location. There was plenty to pick up. The challenge was to distinguish the products of wild animals from those of domestic animals. Roland looked at one slightly bleached tootsie-roll on the ground and said, "Dog. Don't you think that looks like dog?" For just a few of the more meaningful turds, he brought out a small paper bag and captured the matter. Then he pulled a GPS unit from the backpack, read out the location, and marked the bag with place and time. Before we went on, everything—the marker, the paper bag with the turd, and the GPS unit went back into his pack. After I had spent a certain amount of time with Roland, I was no longer surprised by what he might stuff into or withdraw from his backpack. His line of work required him to be just as comfortable with shit as he was with satellite signals and digital readouts, and he was quite resourceful. If what he needed was coyotes for lab analysis, he made it a point to get to know the trappers who were successful.

Roland was laying the groundwork for a study that as yet lacked a design. What he had to do now was frame the most important questions about the Pine Bush coyotes and figure out a system that would turn up the data to answer them. He was open to all possibility.

He was accumulating locations for a kind of scat map of several tracts of pine barrens. This, along with his observations of tracks and a couple of camera traps he had set out—one a few yards from a friend's flagstone patio—would give him some notion of where the coyotes and other animals were hanging out and what food might attract them. We were prospecting sites for the traps that would go out that winter. But it seemed improbable to me that Roland could actually trap and collar any coyotes here, no matter what the bait, because it seemed like an improbable place for a coyote to live. The houses, the landscaping, the stores and offices just over the next low rise—it didn't seem wild enough for wild animals. Furthermore, we had walked all morning and had never gotten away from the noise of the thruway. But he was confident about the presence of animals.

"You know, there are even fisher here," he said. The fisher is a large, aggressive member of the weasel family with a dark fur as luxurious as a mink's and an enthusiasm for killing that doesn't stop even at a porcupine. It lives in the relatively untouched pine and hardwood forests of the North, and in New York it has been thought to confine itself to the Adirondacks. But he said, "I found a body print where one had dropped down from a tree next to the bait for one of the camera traps—that was a big one. Then we got its picture." Evidence of a fisher in coyote territory, he said, begged a question, "Are there links between a coyote and a fisher?"

Was this an important question? And was it an important question for him, Roland Kays, to be trying to answer at this point in his career?

"Depends on whether or not I do a good study on it," he said.

"Good science" was something that had come up often in my conversations with scientists. But when I asked exactly what constituted good science, they seemed hard put to define the standard. It was too generally understood and internalized.

Bad science was not so difficult. Stories proliferated. One of these came from Roland. When he was in Panama studying kinkajous, another scientist working in the same rain forest plot was carrying out a study of a species of antwren, keeping track of nests and production. She happened to spot a snake winding up a tree toward one of the nests she was documenting. She killed the snake.

"What's the problem with that?" I could see that the researcher was interfering with the eat-and-be-eaten process of nature and with the process she was studying, but I wanted to get Roland's thoughts on her behavior.

"Not good science," he said without reference to eat-and-be-eaten. "That's just not good science."

When it came to wildlife research, I asked Roland, would a study of an exotic animal be considered better than a study of an animal close to home? Would Roland's work on kinkajous in Panama be considered more important than his research on coyotes in Albany?

The question slowed him down a little. He's quick, but he's not hasty, and he's serious about the need to be right.

"No," he decided, "it might be more *fun* for the scientist to work in the tropics or the Arctic, but really the quality of the work depends on whether or not you're asking interesting questions and are able to some extent to answer them."

By asking a question or two, framing a hypothesis, and setting the traps, Roland would actually lay a trap for himself. Whatever information the trap yielded must, to some extent, satisfy his questions and add to the body of existing knowledge of the animal.

"Are there questions you can ask about coyotes in the Pine Bush that are more interesting than the questions in your work on kinkajous?"

"Maybe not *more* interesting—remember, there were some physical and technical challenges in the Panama research—but there are definitely questions we can address here that are just *as* interesting scientifically.

"One question that has important implications for conservation—how do mammals, particularly carnivores, which tend to require more land, divvy up the space in what are already small territories?" In the tight, fractured confines of the Pine Bush, I could immediately see the conservation implications of more than one kind of animal living in the same place, what Roland referred to as *sympatry*. It matters how much space a coyote requires, but it matters more how many other animals the same piece of land will support.

"And behavior," he went on. "How is the evolution of behavior affected by the increased proximity to humans?" Maybe a fisher in an Albany backyard indicated the animal is more flexible about where it lives and what it eats than it had been given credit for. "That's a question that we need to look at for the long term. I mean if you think about it—*behavior* and *survival*." Roland proposed this link speculatively. Depending on the preliminary information he came up with, the question might or might not structure his research.

The coyote is the subject of a sizable literature. This is partly due to how long people have been aware of the coyote and partly to how common the animal is. Its numbers are strong enough to cause the coyote to be labeled a nuisance and targeted for "management." Whatever questions Roland posed for himself were likely to be follow-ons to the basic natural history of the coyote. This does not mean they would be less important, just more specifically targeted. In fact, I found his questions about the little islands of uninhabited pine barrens around Albany more ambitious than those of a researcher working in an uninhabited area, say Gary Roemer during his first round of research on Santa Cruz Island, because they force Roland to account for human activities in the area.

In a sense, the central question about coyotes and the other carnivores in the Pine Bush, what all the other questions boiled down to, was, How do they divvy up with space with the humans? With roads and cars, the expanding disruption of new buildings going up, the diseases carried by pet animals, how do they manage? Or do they manage better because of unintended consequences of our activities?

These are not questions about coyote survival because coyotes have been quite successful almost anywhere they live. They are really questions about how the presence of humans and human works are likely to affect the wild animals we are unaware of. These questions are very difficult because they require consideration of what humans do, and that is why the questions that drove Roland's research were so ambitious. With humans involved, the number of wild-card variables shoots up.

We came off the trail and drove away from the Pine Bush, around the back side of Albany. I noticed a black dot between the collar of Roland's parka and his gold earring.

"Are you concerned that you have a tick on your neck?"

He looked annoyed. His hands were taken up with driving. "Would you get it off?" At the next stoplight, he looked down at the bench seat beside him and between his legs, and he began sweeping it with his hand. The tick had plenty of company. At another pause in traffic, he looked me over carefully but didn't see any ticks.

"Seems like the wrong time of year to be picking them up out on the trail," I suggested.

"Yeah," he said. "It's the coyotes in back."

The freezer locker was in the relic of an old brick warehouse alongside some railroad tracks, and I wondered how Roland had found this place that would accept dead coyotes. A man rolled a dolly to the edge of the loading dock, and Roland hauled out the first box of carcasses. When the second carton came out and the two men tried to stack it on top of the one already on the dolly, the lid came off and the animals in their clear plastic body bags slid out of the box. The moment turned surreal: I had started this quest on horseback watching a coyote returning from the hunt, and I had ended up on an industrial back street in a tick-infested truck owned by the State of New York with a man who was intent on capturing coyote shit and delivering dead coyotes to a freezer locker. I thought, "This work is bizarre." Roland's job is to take the odd fact of nature from whatever raw evidence comes to hand and to find the relevance of that fact to the sophisticated facades of civilized knowledge—and he addresses this task like play. He thinks it's fun.

Taking no notice of the contents of the bags, the locker worker wrestled the carcasses back into the box and handed Roland a form to sign. Evidently he had taken other deliveries from the guy from the museum.

Roland brushed off the truck seat and climbed in, starting the motor and slamming the door at the same time. He knew this rustedout district. He navigated its back streets automatically, and we talked about going to Panama to see the kinkajous—he had some ideas, who to contact, cool places to go and things to do. He enjoyed thinking about another project with the possibility of more play. When we reached the silver diner, what the day had yielded was shit and coyote carcasses.

"How many coyotes have you seen in the Pine Bush?"

"Me personally? None—yet." He wasn't troubled by that. He was confident the coyotes were there and that he would get the information he was after. He didn't seem worried about the trapping. He was fresh from his work in Panama, where he had been quite successful trapping kinkajous. The animal the Panamanians call *mono de noche,* or night monkey, had eluded researchers for at least a century, but Roland had caught and collared entire families of them. Other researchers had tried to capture the animals on the ground. Roland, however, raised the game off the forest floor—as I said, he is resourceful. Borrowing a technique from earlier tree-trapping studies that had lifted mouse-size traps into trees, he used a slingshot to shoot fishing line over a high branch, and then he used the fishing line to draw a heavier rope over the branch. The rope would haul up a good-sized cage trap and suspend it a hundred feet above the rain forest floor. If the slingshot failed to carry the line to the right place, Roland shinnied up to that place. The traps were set where the kinkajous lived, and they caught kinkajous.

Another factor sustaining Roland's confidence was that now, for the first time, he wasn't working alone. He had the regular help of a field assistant, a graduate student named Dan Bogan, who had worked at trapping coyotes before. They would trap the animals, put radio collars on them, and then track them. They would find out what he needed to know.

The next morning there was an e-mail from Roland: "Sorry about the ticks. Did you have any problems?"

Only four or five on my back.

In spite of the tick-infested coyote corpses, I was enjoying the preliminaries to trapping, hiking, scouting locations, picking up scat, rigging camera traps, getting Roland's ideas as the work proceeded. I hadn't yet dealt with a live, caught animal, but I had found I could at least deal with dead ones. I could see there was an intellectual component to these stubbornly practical activities: the process of figuring out how to trap the animals also influenced the design of his research. It helped him decide which questions he could answer if his trapping was successful.

Roland's challenge was to ask a question that would be meaningful and to be reasonably sure that the data the trap would capture would help answer it. Understandably, it is often the case that the questions shrink with the realities in the field. "Usually," Todd Fuller said, "you start with the broadest study that seems possible, and usually you have to narrow the focus." One of his students who wanted to work on jaguars in a preserve in Costa Rica laid out his research design and then had to respond to criticism from his dissertation committee about the scope of the study. Three jaguars? That was it, collar just three jaguars? Fuller intervened with a question. "How many jaguars do you think there are in the park?" "Three." The student had cast as wide a net as was realistic. In the end, he was able to collar only one jaguar, but data from that one cat turned out to be sufficient to produce new information about the dietary flexibility of the jaguar.

In spite of the high-technology components of his preparations, the camera surveillance and the GPS map of scat deposits, Roland's approach to trapping coyotes was rudimentary: find a likely spot, set a trap, catch a coyote and collar it. In contrast, Gary Roemer's scheme for trapping the Channel Island foxes was highly systematic and involved repeated trapping of the same foxes. The surprisingly docile nature of the Channel Island fox made the fairly elaborate trapping scheme possible. It would not be feasible for Roland to approach trapping coyotes in the Pine Bush with the same rigor. First, there was already a grid, the one put in place by humans. The two highways, the state roads, and the cross-streets splintered the landscape and exerted considerable control on the coyotes' movements. It would have been pointless to superimpose a geometrical scheme on the fragments of the preserve as if they were untouched wilderness. Second, there was the very different character of the coyote. The Island foxes were naïve about humans and the threats they posed. The coyotes were able to survive in suburban Albany because they were savvy about the dangers of humans.

I had no firsthand knowledge of trapping, but still, I wondered how it would go for Roland in the Pine Bush. The place, with its office buildings and housing spores, seemed unlikely, and tricky, and Roland wasn't seeing many coyotes. In fact, he wasn't seeing as many as I was. Partly this was a matter of terrain and partly a matter of coyote genius. Where I live, a coyote often has to cross open land to find food. In the Pine Bush, a coyote hardly has room to work up to a lope between cross-streets—and because of this the Pine Bush is a perfect backdrop for the coyote's signature talent for camouflage.

When the toddler in the Pecos Bill legend was adopted by a pack of coyotes, his very first lesson in coyotehood—the most important thing the little boy-coyote had to learn in order to become a coyote—was "the rigid pose of invisibility." It would allow the apprentice to see everything without being seen, and it allows real coyotes to be in the picture but escape from view. I once mistook a pair of coyotes for two fence posts. They were standing completely exposed to view in verdant new-mown alfalfa at the end of a field. They were perfectly still. For the coyotes in the Pine Bush, where the landscape-cityscape around Albany was visually complicated, it would be even easier to converge with the background.

Another factor that was probably limiting Roland's coyote sightings was that during daylight hours, the Pine Bush is completely taken over by humans, and I suspect this caused the coyotes to restrict their travels to the hours of darkness more rigorously than the Finger Lakes coyotes.

At this early stage of his research, his lack of personal sightings wasn't discouraging Roland. Neither was the fact that he had not yet worked with an animal whose survival depended on an awareness of humans and their habits or with an animal so profoundly informed by scent. In the late fall, he and Dan used the scat map and camera trap photos to locate the traps. Then they waited. Dan checked the traps early every day. This was to minimize the time any coyote they might catch spent in the trap. Sometimes Roland went with him. As winter approached they were still waiting.

The Pine Bush coyotes proved more difficult to trap than Roland and even Dan had anticipated. They were hardly the first coyote researchers to experience frustration, and many of their difficulties had nothing do with the fact that they were trapping in the Pine Bush. Gary Goff, who worked in a wilder area in the Adirondack foothills north of Albany in the 1970s, reported spending more than five hundred nights trapping. He collared two coyotes. I reported this figure to Roland, and he said, "I'm not surprised." He was already wising up, recalculating his own opportunities. Catching coyotes was going to take some time.

After winter set in hard and there had been a number of snowfalls, making food harder for the coyotes to come by, Roland and Dan succeeded in trapping and collaring three coyotes, two of them female. Telemetry was commencing, and trapping would continue.

They called a halt early in the spring. This was to allow any pregnant female coyotes to whelp, sometime in March, and to start their pups off in peace and quiet. In late April, an e-mail from Roland announced that one of the collared females had pups. He sent me the video clip, the product of a new digital videocam. It was a dreamlike sequence of gray shapes moving against a background only slightly lower on the grayscale. He said that, judging from the number of shapes bumbling around the opening of the den he and Dan had located, there were definitely four and probably five pups.

"How exciting!" I burbled. "You've actually seen them."

"Only on the video," he cautioned me. "We've got the videocam mounted near the den, and we're getting some pretty good stuff."

Evidently not good enough. By the time I drove up to the Pine Bush to see the den a few days later, the news was that Roland had scared the mother coyote and she had moved her pups. My excitement faded considerably when I learned that the day would be devoted to trapping errands instead of infant coyotes. I drove to the silver diner to meet Roland and Dan. The scene along Route 20 had changed subtly since my last visit. A new drive opening to the big

Crossgates Mall, a new shop added to an existing shopping plaza, expanded parking here and there, another fast-food place I hadn't noticed on my first visit. The coyotes' competition was on the move.

Dan was younger than Roland and easily a match for him in terms of physical fitness and drive. His shaved head bristled with tiny hairs, and he had bright blue eyes and a direct gaze. He didn't say much. I thought maybe he was shy, what people around here call backward, but I've learned that what appears to be reticence is reflection. He doesn't offer up or respond quickly in conversation because he is one of the rare people who actually thinks before he speaks.

"I got greedy," Roland explained about the mother coyote moving her pups. The video left in doubt enough details that he wanted to try for a closer shot. He climbed up a young hardwood quite close to the den. It was only about eight inches in diameter at its base. He held himself in place by wrapping his legs around the skinny trunk, making like a pretzel, and he dropped a line down to Dan standing in a tangle of equipment below. He hauled up the camera the way he hauled up the kinkajou traps. He almost had it strapped in its new position when a wind came up.

The little tree swayed, and Roland swayed with it. The wind grew stronger, and Roland rode it out. He stayed with the tree until it arched over and brought him and the equipment clattering to the ground. The commotion of people and equipment outside her lying place was too much for the mother coyote. That night she transferred the pups, one by one, to a new den site. Because of the radio collar, Roland knew where she was, but he wasn't about to track down her and her pups again. "I just can't harass her any more."

So he was repurposing the videocam, and our job was to move it from the tree where it was focused on the abandoned hole in the sand to a prospective site for a real trap. Its images would give Roland and Dan a notion of how many coyotes ventured through the area and how many traveled together. Roland would go along with us in the morning to help stake out a new camera site and break down the existing one. Then he would go off to the museum in the afternoon, and Dan and I would get bait and relocate the camera.

Moving the camera was hardly as simple as that phrase suggests. The video trap provided more sophisticated surveillance than a trap that triggered a still camera, but it was an elaborate setup, a testament to the pleasure Roland takes in gadgets. He seems to look at any emerging commercial technology in terms of how it can be exploited for his work, and he doesn't seem to mind the endless tinkering it takes to find out what the new gizmo will produce.

The video needed to run night and day, and to store the constant feed of information, it needed to be digital. It also needed a power source. For this it was connected to a heavy battery pack buried in dead leaves at the base of the tree. The electricity to feed the battery was supplied by a solar cell about a yard square. The solar cell was suspended in a place where an opening in the treetops would let in sunshine. It was a cumbersome invention, a big, stationary cannon for a fleet mark.

The video camera was now hanging from high branches in a stand of mostly young trees. To get the videocam in one of them meant another climb up a flimsy stalk, but Roland seems to enjoy the struggle of hauling himself up something that offers nothing to help the ascent. This, he told me, is something that started in childhood, when he and his younger brother would put on puffy snowsuits and go out into the Michigan winter to work their way up a couple of big pines in their yard. Then they would bounce down, limb by limb. Later, in preparation for his research on kinkajous, he took a course in technical climbing at the Organization for Tropical Studies in Costa Rica. A young hardwood in the Pine Bush posed no problem. He shinnied up, the tree quivering as he went, detached the camera, and let it down.

We brought the solar cell down from the branches just over our heads, coiled up the parachute cord and wires, and hauled it all back out to the road. Dan crawled under the cap of his pickup and made space for the equipment near the cab wall. He was reserving the area near the tailgate for the bait, a necessity I had not yet confronted.

"How old did they say it was?" he asked Roland about the deer carcass the town road crews had delivered to the Department of Environmental Conservation.

"A day or so, I guess."

More dead things.

"Is it bloated?"

Roland shrugged. He had to leave for the museum.

Dan and I drove back out of the Pine Bush and through the outskirts of Albany. Dan had come to work for Roland from a coyote-stalking project in suburban Illinois, and when he moved East, his father helped him adapt the state truck for telemetry, installing an antenna on the roof of the truck. Inside the cab there was a handle on the ceiling, and when you shifted the handle, the antenna on top of the truck swung. The British biologist David Macdonald used cars with similar adaptations to carry out his pioneering radio-location study of the foxes of suburban Oxford.

We pulled up to the building that housed the DEC incinerator, and the biologist who met us rolled up the overhead door. We had our choice of dead deer. On the cement floor in front of the incinerator were the bodies of six or seven deer the highway crews had picked up in various states of decomposition. Dan looked them over, and again I was struck by how bizarre this appraisal might be under ordinary circumstances: how tempting was each carcass in its particular state of decay? Dan picked up one, pinning two legs in each fist, and threw it onto the truck bed. Nothing about this seemed to bother him. He was strong enough that the deer's weight caused him only a little effort, and he was inured to the stench. I was not inured. I tried not to breathe. Stench is what would draw a coyote.

We drove the deer carcass to a patch of Pine Bush not far from an intersection where office buildings occupied two corners. It was se-cluded enough to foster coyote traffic and yet not so far off the road to make it difficult to haul in a dead deer. Dan parked the truck once, then turned it around and parked it in another place, where he thought his activities would be less likely to attract attention.

"You mean people will actually stop and ask you what you're doing?"

"Sometimes it isn't just people. I've had the police stop me."

"Do they believe your story?"

"I guess."

Under the pickup cap, along with the dead deer and the video equipment, there were rubber gloves, syringes, and a tranquilizer called Telozol, a long stick as worn as a walking stick with a deep *Y* at one end, and leg-hold traps. Dan demonstrated one of these traps. It was a daunting machine, a metal plate armed with heavy springs that triggered two steel arcs, the jaws. If the trap were correctly tuned up, the jaws snapped when the coyote brought a crucial amount of its weight to bear on the metal plate. The jaws were padded, but the animal-catching machine made me nervous.

"Pretty grim-looking."

Dan said, "You know, these aren't that bad. A lot of people don't like them—I guess because of the way they look—but they're really pretty safe." He knew the term was relative, and he used *safe* to apply only to animals trapped for research. When he found a coyote in one of his traps, he used the forked stick to pin the neck of the animal. The stick held the animal down while he injected it with the Telozol. While the coyote was unconscious, he took its vital statistics and fit it with a tattletale radio collar. Then he waited until it stirred and became fully awake. Maybe the coyote came to and sprinted out of the cage with no more than a sore leg and a headache.

I was relieved not to be involved with setting out a real trap, a leg-hold or snare. That would have been a much simpler project, but—even if it was for the overall benefit of that coyote and its kind—I wasn't sure how I would feel about the prospect of seeing a caught coyote. This was, of course, just what Roland and Dan wanted to see. The two men were used to finding an animal in a trap and dealing with its distress. To them, the video images and the animal with the jackhammer pulse were of a piece, just different ways to get at the answers.

Dan put on the rubber gloves but left the leg-hold trap, the stick, and the syringes in the truck. We slid the deer off the tailgate and started up the bank toward the trees with it. To my amazement, I was able to take hold of two legs and help tote the leaden carcass. I was becoming part of this weird line of work. We stopped to catch our breath and then in another surge of effort lugged the deer into the trees, through some brush, and down into a low swale between two sand hills.

Although the trap we were setting wouldn't physically arrest a coyote, it had to be prepared with the same care. The bait, the deer carcass a bit more bloated from travel in the heat under the truck cap, was reliably inviting. But the invitation couldn't be qualified by anything off-putting about its location, appearance, or, especially, smell, and the invitation had to stay in place. Still wearing the gloves, Dan used a light cable and metal stake to rivet the carcass in place. The gloves were not to keep the scent of the dead deer off him. They were to keep his scent off the deer.

It was hard to believe that the olfactory system of any living creature, no matter how acute, could tease out of the air in this patch of
Pine Bush any scent except rotting deer. But many researchers and
writers have pointed out that the world of the carnivores is ordered by
scent. In the case of the canids, animals in the dog family, their re-
liance on scent is extreme. The odors they leave in urine, feces, and
the excretions of various glands carry information on the whereabouts
and land claims of other competing animals and on potential breeding partners. For a coyote or any other animal that needs large areas
to roam in and that likes to travel alone, a heightened awareness of
odors allows it to avoid trouble. A coyote is led through life by its
nose.

I asked about the scent my own unprotected hands had left in
rings around the deer's fetlocks.

He shrugged. "It's good to be careful, but you never can tell. Last
week when it was hot like this, I got disorganized and left stuff home,
broke all the rules. I was setting out traps wearing shorts, sweating, no
gloves. And those traps caught two coyotes." No doubt the coyotes
had caught his scent, but for some reason—perhaps the distraction of
other scents and sounds or hunger—they disregarded the information. Whatever the circumstances, they might or might not repeat
themselves when it came to my scent on the dead deer's lower legs.

I realized that it wasn't only Roland who was setting a trap for himself. In a way, by coming along and helping out with the trapping
errands, I had set a trap for myself. I wasn't sure what I thought about
interfering with a wild animal, much less killing it, as is necessary in
some lines of research, to get information about the animal. It was
nervousness about meddling with nature. I have often felt it a failure
that my religious beliefs seem to be limited to an awe of nature. But
this is as close to faith as I can get, and I was jittery about transgress-
ing on something put in place by a larger power. Before I had a chance
to sort out my thinking, I was involved.

Our video trap would put the coyotes in no immediate danger,
but if the videocam recorded enough coyotes passing through, Roland and Dan were likely to replace the camera with a leg-hold trap.
That would be a different story. Even in cases like the Pine Bush where
biologists are trapping with the best possible intentions, there are risks
to that trapped animal. This is true of leg-hold traps, pitfall traps that

hold whatever animals tumble in and can't crawl out, cage traps that confine the animal—any trap that arrests the animal. The animal cannot be left in the trap too long. Panic can cause it to fling itself around or to chew off the part of its body holding it to the trap, and weather can take its toll on an animal that can't move. To prevent casualties, the traps must be checked regularly and promptly.

The dangers to wild animals being handled during research have been widely discussed. The American Society of Mammalogists and most universities and conservation societies have codes of conduct governing the treatment of wildlife research subjects, and most research institutions have an oversight committee similar to those that oversee experiments with human subjects. But in spite of these safeguards, there is no way for a scientist to anticipate all animal behavior, all freak weather, all potential consequences for a trapped animal. Accidents happen, and many researchers have stories that cause them pain to remember. Alan Rabinowitz, whose work on jaguars in Belize eventually resulted in the creation of a refuge for the big cats, experienced a long period of frustration trying to trap a jaguar. Then one of his first captures went badly wrong. The jaguar tried to bite its way out of the cage trap and broke both of its canine teeth, rendering itself helpless. Elise told me she had caught a tiny wild cat called the kodkod in a leg-hold trap set for a Darwin's fox, and by the time she could release it, the little cat, which gets its living by climbing trees and killing birds, had gnawed off part of its toes. A student working for Roland on Barro Colorado Island in Panama accidentally killed an ocelot with an overdose of sedative. Roland accepted responsibility for the death, which, because it occurred on Barro Colorado, an ecological preserve, was likely to be viewed with more alarm than if the cat had died on mainland Panama. Accidents like these are always taken quite seriously by the research community, and while a scientist like Roland might enjoy the strategic challenges of trapping, none of those I spoke with participated in trapping because they enjoyed working up animal subjects.

"I didn't *like* darting the lions," George Schaller told me about the procedure he used extensively in the Serengeti. "The only time I have used a method like this is when there was no other way to get the data." As I thought further about the leg-hold trap rattling around in the back of Dan's pickup, I realized that this sort of triage—a decision to sedate or a decision to trap—is unavoidable if the study itself is, by virtue of the questions it poses, necessary.

For some studies intended to answer certain kinds of questions, there are a number of "noninvasive" techniques for getting information indirectly, like camera traps, track boxes, and hair snags. These are put to use most often in broad survey work. Only slightly more sophisticated than Darwin's ride-out-and-shoot forays from the *Beagle,* this kind of research reveals the same sort of information: which species live in a given area and how numerous the animals might be.

During the time he was tracking coyotes in the Pine Bush, Roland also cooperated with Justina Ray, of the Wildlife Conservation Society, and Matt Gompper, now of the University of Missouri, on a large-scale survey of carnivores in the Adirondack Park. The study was a big, relatively fast project. It took in a big piece of the park, and it had a staff of three scientists and five research assistants. The park is three times the size of Greater Yellowstone, and the team selected an interior chunk that included the High Peaks and the flatter areas north and south of them. They designed the survey area so that the shallows of civilization lapped at its edges. Their idea was to move quickly and, using noninvasive techniques such as scat collection, camera traps, and track plates, take a rough census of the carnivores, particularly the coyotes. They wanted to get some notion of which animals are in which parts and in which kinds of terrain and what their numbers might be. This could reveal how the different carnivores divided up the turf and responded to the presence of human populations. Their sampling of the park's carnivore inhabitants answered an essential question about any region: which animals are there to be protected?

It did not attempt, however, to answer questions about why the animals live where they do, questions about the animals' needs and habits. To answer those questions, you have to be able to get your hands on an animal long enough to mark it in some way.

When I mentioned to Roland a carnivore biologist who was opposed to touching the animals she studied, he said, "But how much would we know about most of these animals if we never interfered with them? And how many of these animals would be gone without our knowing anything about them?"

His questions were impossible to answer, even for a good bio-statistician, and they went straight to the concerns that had been bubbling under my experiences in the field. I was all for the mission, but I worried about the things it takes to immobilize a wild animal. I tried to put the dangers in perspective: It is clear that the riskiness to the animals of the activities of scientists is rather minor when it is contrasted with the perils posed by ordinary people—guns, automobiles, roads, and, witness the Albany Pine Bush, their penchant for tearing up undisturbed land. Furthermore, a research project might be useful in protecting animals from these forms of human obliviousness, and this should justify some calculated risk to the animals under study. But even when this is the case, I decided, the information a trapped animal produces, each datum from each collar, has to be worth the risk of its getting. Roland has to ask questions worth answering, and the data from the live traps that follow the video trap that Dan and I were setting had not only to answer them but to eventually help the coyotes.

Dan proceeded with his usual caution, in spite of the possible deterrent of my scent already on the deer carcass. He covered the stake and cable with dry leaves, and when we had hoisted the solar cell into place and positioned the camera, we added more leaves and brush to camouflage the battery parked at the base of a tree. We looked through the videocam's viewer and decided the scene was set perfectly. We left the videocam running in the sandy hollow a mile or so south of the thruway. Whether or not a coyote or more than one coyote would slip into the range of the videocam remained to be seen.

The coyote's life proceeds risky moment by risky moment, and survival is the result of a complicated balancing of risk and reward. For the coyote, which is currently top predator in the Pine Bush, the risks were disease, to some extent other coyotes, but primarily people—cars, traps, guns, and poison. Ironically, it was also people and their attitudes that were causing trouble for Roland and Dan. If they weren't much aware when they began the coyote project that people are monkey wrenches waiting to be thrown into the works, Roland and Dan were discovering that in hard terms. The Pine Bush coyotes were being shot, trapped, and killed by cars so frequently that

Dan was challenged to keep enough of his collared animals alive long enough to document anything about them.

Dan was quite stoic about the frustrations, and considering that he worked mostly alone traveling the Pine Bush at odd hours, I found this admirable. He had spoken about girls, a couple of different girls, and I wondered if his work with its crazy hours and intense odors didn't put off the women. I was curious about how he felt about his job just then, when the coyotes were proving tricky to trap and the ones who were not wily enough to avoid the radio collars were also not wily enough to avoid the many dangers of suburbia.

"If you meet someone at a party," I asked him, "do you tell her what you actually do?" With the truck with the antenna on the roof and the bait and scent jars, the rubber gloves and syringes and Telozol. "Or do you just say you do research?"

Dan smiled, steady and reflective as usual. There is something so forthright about him, so genuine in himself that he has the effect of making me feel like a fraud for asking questions like this. He said, "I tell them what I do. Sometimes they don't believe me—one guy said, 'Oh right, you just hang out those snares, set out those traps, and the coyotes just walk right in.'"

"What did you say?"

He nodded, still smiling. "Said, 'Yes. That's right. They just walk right in.'"

"These animals," Roland told an ornithologist friend at dinner one night, "are hard as shit to catch."

Because their hunting is what keeps coyotes on the move, trapping turns the process of predation inside-out. Coyotes are never out rambling for the pleasure of taking the air, and although sexual urges may drive a coyote during breeding season, the usual force behind its travel routine is hunger.

When I first encountered the coyote carrying the dead rabbit, I was intrigued by the violence that put the carcass in its jaws. I don't think there was anything unusual about my startled speculations. Even scientists refer to the big predators, the tigers and lions and wolves, as "charismatic." Part of the charisma has to do with the capacity to kill ruthlessly and part from spectacular stalk-and-chase scenes we associate with this capacity. I suspect that many of us wonder if some part of the tiger or wolf survives in us. We wonder if there are links between predation of animals, our hunting, and our violence against each other. At the time I met up with the coyote, I had been troubled by a couple of local murders, real coroner's specials. Both were horrific multiple murders that ended in fire to erase the grisly damage to the bodies, and I worried about the impulses that drove the violence. Where did these come from?

Enough carcasses, enough hairs teased out of fox shit, and that question receded. Not that it isn't a very important question. But traveling with Roland made it clear that even among wild carnivores, murder is something quite different than predation. The mechanism that set the coyote on the rabbit and would draw a coyote close to Dan's video trap is routine hunger. It is true that coyotes and foxes and their canid brethren wolves, African hunting dogs, and dholes, can and do turn on each other and fight like the sons of bitches they are. But these are instances of social aggression, and in comparison with the routine killings of predation they are relatively infrequent. It seems possible to me that animal murders in response to competition or to some silent genetic goal are in fact connected to the most primitive sources of human violence. But as I think about the most shocking kinds of human violence, I have to credit humans with a number of capacities that are not, so far as we know, equaled by other higher animals: almost infinite physical dexterity, detailed memory, and the expanded imagination to apply both to the task of killing.

I came to another conclusion about the process of eat-and-be-eaten. It is of necessity very repetitive. The story of predation is the same movie run over and over. When I asked Alan Rabinowitz about his well-known work with charismatic cats, he expressed a similar view of the process of predation. His reason for devoting so much time to top predators is that each holds down a lot of territory, and that territory houses many other species. He said, "You know big cats really aren't that interesting. They hunt, they gorge, they sleep."

What keeps the constantly recurring plot from being boring to a biologist is the variety of animal strategies for and styles of killing. Just how the hunt proceeds and how the kills are made are usually among the first recorded observations of a predatory animal. Cataloging almost everything that had been reported about the carnivore family, R. F. Ewer was usually able to include, in her encyclopedic work *The*

Carnivores, information about hunting and killing. She was fond of the term "occipital crunch," which described the method by which the weasels snap the head of the victim back against its spine. Cats also use this technique, but for larger targets, such as a wildebeest or a zebra, they often go for the throat, setting their teeth there, clamping down and eventually suffocating the quarry. Animals like the African hunting dog that hunt in groups run down their prey, snatch onto convenient tooth-holds to drag it down, and then simply begin eating through the prone animal, starting with the softest parts under the tail. On a frigid winter day I found a fresh deer carcass in the snow. It was wreathed by coyote prints, and its hindquarters had been eaten out. The next morning, only the head, neck, and parts of its shoulder were still untouched, and after several days, only bones and a few blood-clotted clumps of hair were left.

Fear and learning are key forces in the process of predation. Birds that live on uninhabited islands often have no fear of humans, and animals that live in the absence of predators tend to lose their fear response. Reading accounts and watching film sequences of hunting by lions, wolves, and wild dogs hunting herds of animals, I have often been struck by how little commotion is caused by the appearance of a capable predator approaching the herd. A few of the grazing animals— antelope, zebra, wildebeest—might lift their heads to note the arrival of the potential killer, but often there is no panic, no sudden rush away from the killer. The predator closes in, and at this point the herd may begin moving away. Or it may not. In a minute or so one of their number may be on the ground being disemboweled. I was surprised by this passivity. It seemed fatalistic—"Oh, well, bound to go sometime."

When I asked George Schaller about wildebeest behaving this way in the presence of lions, he pointed out that alarm and flight take a lot out of each animal in the herd and that every lion a wildebeest sees is not necessarily a hungry lion. For herd animals, a more active response to the arrival of a potential killer would keep the animals in a nearly constant state of adrenaline surge. The animals can't keep up that level of emotional response, and so they learn to read predator behavior. "Think of it like being in traffic in Manhattan," he advised me. "You are aware of all the cars around you, but you can't worry about each one of them. You worry about the ones you have learned to have reason to worry about." The wildebeests flee from only the lions that they judge a serious enough threat to justify the expense of their energy.

Coyotes probably are as canny as we give them credit for being. But occasionally, by accident or not, they come into our presence, and when they do they often appear unconcerned about that fact. I suspect that what humans see as bold and nonchalant is a matter of animal focus. The animal has some place it needs to get to, and it has accepted the risks that go with its route at that particular time of day. It may be this focus that draws a coyote into a trap. Sometimes animals get caught in traps because they wander into them without perceiving the setup. But I suspect that usually the animal senses something unusual and for some reason—hunger, fatigue, young waiting in a den—needs to take the risk. The trick to successful trapping is to make the risk acceptable to the animal.

If a coyote crossed the street and caught a whiff of the dead deer in our trap and followed it over the crest of the sand hill, would it look down on the scene Dan and I had so carefully wrought and detect the videocam, the solar cell, the cable and stake, and a vaguely human odor? If it did, would the gizmos and the scent warn it off? Or would it gaze down on the untouched carcass and believe itself a suddenly lucky dog?

As it worked out, a rotting deer carcass was not necessarily the key to trapping coyotes. Dan began having some success with scent, the social glue for many carnivore species, and manufactured scent proved too tantalizing for one young coyote to resist.

I was on my way to Albany because Dan had discovered another litter of coyote pups. This time the mother was not collared. Dan had simply come upon the den on one of his rambles.

"Tomorrow is the big day," Dan declared in the instructions he e-mailed to me and a good number of friends in Albany. "I'm planning on tagging coyote pups and will need some help! I'm looking to you guys for an extra hand for digging, handling pups: ear tagging, weighing, sexing, checking general health and special pelage markings. I'll be the one actually going into the den, so I'll need people above ground to handle pups. . . . Don't wear any stinking perfume or clothes. Bring a pair of clean cotton gloves if you can. If not, we'll use latex. Anything is better than stinky human hands. Plan on being quiet, and patient. There is a chance that the parents have switched dens in the past few days, so I may have to look around for the new den."

The evening before his well-planned raid, Dan found the den empty. The female had somehow gotten wind of—coyotes have impressed upon me the aptness of this phrase—the humans' interest in her cubs. The fact that she was uncollared meant that tracking her down in her new den would require a lot of effort and vigilance. "I've told him I don't think it's worth the effort," Roland said when he called to tell me the raid was canceled. "And she—the female coyote—is already upset. I think we should concentrate on the adults, trapping and tracking. That's been hard enough."

But it was hard for Dan to give up on this. He returned with some friends to the abandoned den from which the mother coyote had moved her pups. It was a narrow tunnel that wormed its way to a final chamber, which could have been as far as twenty-five feet from the opening. He crawled into the hole while his friends held him by his ankles. Just when he thought he found the chamber, his friends ran out of leg to hold. "It went back in there a pretty good ways." Frustrated, Dan went a step further with Roland's videocam.

"It's my Den Crawler," he announced when he set what looked like a big toy on the concrete floor of a garage owned by the Pine Bush Preserve. It was a toy, I realized, and it looked something like a diminutive tank. With Dan ordering it around the garage floor with a remote-control unit, it crawled along carrying Roland's digital videocamera on its top deck and dragging behind it the cable that connected the videocam to its battery. The little video screen displayed a fun-house view of the concrete, my feet, the hubcap of a truck parked in the building. No doubt this bit of remote-control madness was encouraged by Roland, whose opportunism about technology rivaled the coyotes' about food. It hadn't been tried, it was fun, and it might work. Who knows? The Den Crawler might be documented as a breakthrough in observing animals that den up.

Dan test-drove the Den Crawler by putting it down the same hole he had wriggled into.

"Works pretty good," he reported. "Steers real good and everything. I just got to figure out how to give it a little more range."

A little more range, and coyote mothers all over the Pine Bush would be jerking awake to find their tiny chambers being invaded by a toy tank drawing a bead on them with a big rectangular eye, and what the eye would show was a female coyote nursing pups.

Even though there would be no pups to be seen on the trip to the Pine Bush, I decided to go anyway. It had been a while since I had visited the trapping. Roland came with us that morning to inspect the traps. If he had any expectations, they were certainly muted. The second debacle with pups seemed to have left both him and Dan subdued. A couple of miles from the corner where Dan and I had laid the video trap, Dan suddenly turned his truck into a dirt lane. We followed the lane behind an old farmhouse and then, a hundred yards or so from the road, into an abandoned sand pit.

"Hot diggity—," Dan slowed the truck, "—dog!"

A coyote stood in the first trap. She was a slight gray dog, smaller than the coyote I had ridden up to in the hayfield, and she would not have been immediately obvious in the dry scrub on the sandy floor of the pit. But when she saw the truck so close she started to howl. It was a cry for help. We weren't the kind she had in mind. When she saw us get out of the truck, she began pulling at the chain that held her leg, still crying.

"Stay behind the truck," Roland said sternly as I opened the door. He remained there with me and let Dan manage the captive.

What happened next was remarkable and also unremarkable. Dan took his time, going to the back of the truck, bringing out his forked stick, then the wire cage. Every move was quiet, deliberate, slow motion. He handed off the cage to Roland and advanced carefully on the coyote. Every move said, "I am nothing to be worried about. I am hardly even noticeable." He had a coyote's talent for receding to invisibility. She stopped howling and watched. She remained quiet and tense until he was a couple of yards away. Then she turned to fight him, howling briefly then snarling, lunging against the leg chain. Dan waded in slowly, keeping his eyes on her. Everything about him was slow. He seemed to forget that he had the forked stick to pin her down by the neck. Instead, when she scrambled at him snarling, all teeth, he caught her by a hind leg and in a single move ran his hand up to the scruff of her neck and laid her on her side. In that instant she stopped struggling.

Nothing rough had happened to either of them. Dan laid the stick across her shoulder to her head, and she seemed to think this magic wand was holding her down. Roland came up with the cage, and Dan delivered her into it tail first. They put the cage in the shade of a sumac and left her alone.

When Roland came back to the truck, he went around behind it and advised me to "try to stay out of her sight." Evidently just an awareness of how close we were would be stressful.

"She's pretty small," Dan said, and he went into his tool kit to select a collar.

"She's not a pup," Roland observed.

"Nope. Might not even be young-of-the-year. I don't know what she is, but I'm not sure I've got a collar to fit her."

While Dan was looking around for foam to pad the radio collar, Roland found her tracks in the sand. "Look, you can see how she was just trotting along, and all of a sudden when she caught a whiff of the trap, she did a 180."

"Yeah, it was just scent. No bait," Dan said. "She's the second one I've caught that way."

Roland backtracked and found the tracks of another coyote. Then another. They were clear as linotype text. "She was traveling with a pack, probably her family. They just kept going—look at that—none of them even went over to see what happened to her."

Dan sedated her, and while they waited for the Telozol to take effect, Roland worked with a pocketknife at the fluorescent tape he had laid down in stripes on the collar. He used distinctive Day-Glo patterns to identify individual coyotes in the pictures they triggered with the camera traps. But he and Dan had begun to wonder if the Day-Glo tape was drawing the attention of hunters, and they decided to remove the tape. They talked about girls, the ones Dan could see, the one he was seeing. Roland, being married, was out of the game, just a coach. All I could think was, "I will never be so close to a coyote again unless it's roadkill. I will never be this close again."

When the coyote was completely out, Dan laid her on the tailgate, looked her over to take notes on her teeth and markings, measured her, weighed her, drew blood, and clipped on an ear tag with a tool that looked like pliers.

"How much do you think she weighs?" Dan challenged us.

"Twenty-two pounds," I guessed.

"She's more than that." Dan had, after all, lifted her.

"Usually people guess high because these guys are so fluffy they look bigger than they really are."

She weighed twenty-five pounds. She didn't carry a trace of fat or anything extra. I watched her with great curiosity, trying to fix the details of her coat—which had caught up seed heads from the grass around the trap and a few burrs—and of her oversize feet. These seemed puppylike to me, too big for her leg bones. The hair on her underside was creamy and the skin over her belly surprisingly pale.

The coyote had a deep cut between the pads of one paw, an injury from the trap. Dan was concerned about the cut, but he said, "These guys are pretty tough, and if I try to treat it, it would cause more problems than to let her care for it herself." Then he put her back in the shaded cage. We would leave her alone now and come back after the drug had worn off.

Back in the truck Roland scanned the clipboard. "What about a name?"

"I'm doing a mythology thing." Evidently it was Dan's right to name what he caught, but that didn't stop Roland and me from trying out our ideas.

"Diana."

"Yup."

"Hera."

"Yup."

"Persephone."

He cut us off. "I've got a Web site with some good ones." He wasn't about to give up his prerogative.

When the little coyote came to under the sumac, she might have been a show dog in a travel crate. She had regained herself and kept her dignity. There was hauteur in the way she ignored us. She accepted the fact of her confinement but not the fact that we were anything above her status. She didn't need to look at Dan. His stink filled her nostrils. When he approached the cage, her eyes rolled warily. But she didn't turn her head. As soon as the door fell open, she shot out toward the scrub trees that ringed the sand pit.

"Ouch!" He winced.

"What?"

She was streaking confidently toward the old trees at the north end of the pit.

"That sand going into that cut."

Before Dan's comment was complete, she had vanished in the same direction her family had headed. He named her Diana.

4 ⫷ How to Spot a Fox

I WAS ON MY WAY TO CHILE TO SEE THE DARWIN'S FOX. I HAD not *seen* an Island fox. But laying eyes on the actual animal seemed very important. This was my burden as an amateur, and I was determined to *see* the fox. Darwin's diary, *The Voyage of the Beagle,* made the trip to Chile and the Parque Nacional Nahuelbuta with me. I had sentimental thoughts about having the great man's observations of South America and Chile accompany me, and I wanted to find out what, if anything, he had to say about the fox named after him.

The *Beagle's* mission was to complete the British government's survey of the coast of South America, and Darwin was a paying passenger. Although the ship had already enlisted a surgeon, who would by custom have been in charge of the natural history collection, Darwin was encouraged by a letter from his mentor, J. S. Henslow, to believe the proposed two-year voyage would be a wide-open opportunity for "collecting, observing, and noting anything worthy to be noted in Natural History."

The collecting and classification of all the items brought forth by nature were the heart of natural history. The amateur or incidental naturalist was a primary contributor to these collections and became a stock character, frequently associated with the medical and clerical professions, of the time. Stephen Maturin, the ship's surgeon in Patrick O'Brien's maritime adventure novels, is a wonderful fictional distillation of the role, and there are any number of historical examples of amateurs, including Darwin himself, who made significant contributions to natural science. The Reverend John Bachman, a Lutheran from South Carolina, made many observations of birds, including that of the warbler named after him, and he collaborated on a book on North American mammals with John James Audubon, the father-in-law of both of Bachman's daughters. As famous as Audubon himself would become, he remained an amateur, an avid rambler and observer, until middle age. During the voyage of the *Beagle,* Darwin, who had been pressured by his father into training halfheartedly for both medicine and the clergy, was just beginning to emerge from his status as an amateur.

Collections were formed to serve the goals of science and public knowledge, but also collections of birds and other ornamental products of nature were privately commissioned, bought and sold. Of course, what was gathered in had to be named and assigned a place relative to others of its kind. Tinged with rapaciousness as it was, all this activity recognized the vastness of the natural world and attempted to get a fix on what Darwin referred to as its "productions." Their plenty was a marvel.

One of the productions Darwin brought back to England was a fox. Elise told me he had captured it on Chiloé Island along the southern coast of Chile, and for more than a century that lone specimen and anecdotal evidence that foxes still lived on the island were the sum of scientific knowledge about it. Then, in the 1970s, Chilean biologists observing the foxes on Chiloé heard from park rangers about a similar fox living more than three hundred miles north around the Parque Nacional Nahuelbuta.

That was where I was headed. When my plane landed in Santiago in January, it was high summer there, and in the places in the city where grass had been cultivated the ground was dry and tufted with a bleached thatch. I took the overnight bus south along the Pan-American Highway and, reading Darwin, followed the *Beagle* south along the coast of Argentina to Patagonia and through the Strait of Magellan until the ship was heading in my direction. We met up, so to speak, in Pucón, a small town on the intensely green-blue Lake Villarrica surrounded by volcanoes dramatically capped with snow. I worked on my Spanish and in the process found that the local Chileans not only knew about Darwin but viewed him as a kind of expatriate hero. Other guests at my hostel, who had come to Pucón to trek and to kayak and raft the wild streams that cut along the edges of the volcanoes, mentioned a number of local plants and animals whose common names honored Darwin. "A great man," a waiter told me. "He loved Chile." Whether or not this was accurate, Darwin and the crew of the *Beagle* literally put Chile on the map, and they made an indelible impression on me. I finished *The Voyage of the Beagle* and then read on in Darwin and books about Darwin. C.D., as he often signed his letters—"Believe me, C.D."—became a witness to my reactions and ruminations as I traveled with his contemporary counterparts. He was there, hanging out behind the set, always on my mind but not forthcoming.

The Chileans knew Darwin, but they didn't recognize the name of the land reserve where I was going, Nahuelbuta. Another bus ride took me 240 miles north of Pucón into the Central Valley to Angol, an agricultural center pressed up against the base of the cordillera that separates the Central Valley from the Pacific Ocean.

All along the bus's path through the wheat, pastures, and vineyards in the valley were demonstrations of a determination to modernize and modernize fast: concrete slapped down and propped up to create roads and overpasses, businesses housed in new metal buildings operating without anyone bothering to level the piles of dirt pushed aside to situate the establishments. A driver from CONAF, the Chilean forest service, met me in Angol and explained that Elise had radioed to ask him to drive me to the park. We made the trip up the narrow gravel road to the cordillera in a small Ford truck. Just beyond the city limits of Angol, a mountainside rose abruptly. The arduous climb was made possible by a series of switchbacks, and as the truck ground around one hairpin curve I saw that the mountainside had been denuded by logging. Poised mantis-like on a rocky precipice above our truck was an excavator on crawler tracks. The jaw on the end of its long, jointed neck was grasping at a tree, the last remaining in what had been a stand of radiata pine.

After the long, daunting grade, however, the give and take with the land was more evenhanded. The road moved past small mountain pastures fenced with walls of vertical sticks and separated by dense hedgerows. More mature trees began to take over until, twenty-some miles and more than two hours from Angol, old-growth forest loomed on both sides of the road. A locked gate barred our passage into the park, but almost as soon as our truck pulled up to it, a guardaparque, a park ranger, came down the steps from the gatehouse.

One of Chile's thirty-one national parks, Nahuelbuta is the sanctuary of one of the last remaining stands of ancient trees called araucarias and of a group of Darwin's foxes. Beyond the gate the road was a bare path under the trees. It was as wide as our truck, with wheel ruts that wriggled to dodge the boulders that popped up frequently. Three and a half miles into the park, the road came out into a bowl-shaped meadow, a cove between the mountains. Now that we were in the open I could see the trees that surrounded the meadow.

The araucarias, remarkable survivors from the Jurassic age, are some of the last in the world. All that protects them from the kind of snatch-and-rip logging I saw along the road up from Angol is the park boundaries. Like Santa Cruz, Nahuelbuta is an island. The trees have immense trunks armored with spiny plates that rise branchless for a hundred feet or more before sending out a spray of branches that bear primitive leaves about a foot long. The leaves are sharp enough to cause lacerations like paper cuts, and the thick scales that cover the trunk have similar but less dangerous edges. Some of the araucarias in the park are a thousand years old and, because of the Spanish moss that drapes most of them, look even more ancient.

The grassy hollow was home to Proyecto Zorro, Elise's fox research. Near its rim, set uphill close to the tree line, was a simple one-story gray house with a small deck and stairs that descended to a path that ran down to a flat place in the meadow, where there was a recent ranch structure painted brown-black. Even in daylight it was only the corrugated metal roof that stood out against the brown-black shade under the araucarias. This was the Visitors Center, known to everyone in Proyecto Zorro as the VC.

The driver let me out and turned back for Angol with a cheerful "Listo, listo!" He would be happy to make the two-hour drive again. I found that most of the space in the VC was occupied by an open reception area and visitor restrooms. But in the back, off to one side, was the toehold apartment.

No one answered my knock. I opened the door. The apartment was a dark place, and I was in its narrow entrance hall. This space was jammed with equipment, some of it predictable things made of nylon fabric for camping, other gear that I didn't recognize, and plastic tubs of provisions. There was no one there at the moment or, evidently, in the house up the hill.

In a little while, three people greeted me from the turnaround beside the VC. Kelly Cruce was a long-legged girl in her mid-twenties with a long fall of shiny chestnut hair tacked to the back of her head. On a strap over her shoulder she carried what looked like a boxy transistor radio, and in one hand was a sheaf of collapsible aluminum tubes. In the next two weeks I would spend quite a bit of time with Kelly and her equipment. She was the research assistant currently on duty, and with her were Maura and Jake, two new college graduates who had recently arrived to take over Kelly's job.

Jake was from Colorado, an outgoing person, sturdily built with a thick brush of bright blond hair that twirled out of control in a number of cowlicks. His new colleague Maura was athletic looking and wore the only hairstyle I'd seen since I'd left Pucón that looked intentional. She was just out of Cornell, more reserved than Jake but keen on being in the park. The two of them helped me set my tent on the slope a little north of the VC. I was settling into this bright red, lozenge-shaped shelter when Elise arrived with another woman about her age, a very slim person with pale freckled skin and auburn hair. I expected this would be Kate Doyle, another researcher from the University of Massachusetts who was looking at the park's small mammals—rodents, bats, rabbits—whatever a Darwin's fox might eat. Elise's crutches were gone, but she was still limping noticeably. Right away, before she introduced Kate, she said, "I thought you were coming next week!" She had been preoccupied with the work in the park. "Unfortunately," she mused, "most of us are going to be away for a few days." She would take her truck down to Temuco to be fixed and continue south to errands on Chiloé Island. "But, never mind, you can hang out with Kelly. You'll probably see more than you would sticking with me. She goes all over the park, and she's been here since spring."

Dinner that night was in the gray house up the hill. It was on the Latin American schedule, nine or ten o'clock, prepared and eaten in the light of a couple of candles, a battery-powered lamp, and the glow of propane burners. Nelson Navarro was a guardaparque, and the house was a benefit of his job. He and his wife, Erica, had opened their home to Elise during her first season in Nahuelbuta, and they kept a room for her now on a more or less permanent basis. Their generosity still seemed remarkable to Elise, but she said it wasn't unusual for Chileans. Also, I think that for the "Nelsons," as everyone called the Navarros, Elise relieved the park's isolation. Nelson and Erica were still in their twenties, and for long periods his work in the park kept them from family and friends in Angol and Temuco and from Chile's deter-mined Americanization. Elise brought a bright mind and an intensely American presence into the family, as well as a changing cast of young Americans and pop music from the States. For five-year-old Vanessa, she brought storybooks in English.

Nelson was a handsome, dark-haired man with a dazzling smile. Erica, a small woman with a black ponytail that hung well below her waist, was quieter and not so self-assured around the latest batch of newcomers, Maura and Jake and me. We were joined that night by Christian Muñoz-Donoso, a filmmaker working on a documentary about Nahuelbuta. Nelson kept a fire in the wood stove, which warmed the room and also the water for openly coveted showers. In the hour before the food was set out, a discreet parade of fox re-searchers passed under the Navarros' shower.

We crowded around the table with our backs to the dark. Vanessa and the Americans did most of the talking because Christian and Nel-son and Erica had difficulty following the English. Christian had the light hair and tawny skin the Europeans brought to Chile. He was a quiet person, taciturn by nature, and I think the chatter in English made him even more reticent.

This was the Proyecto Zorro household, gathered in Nahuelbuta's protected patch of trees to collect data on a fox. Elise's work was the first systematic research on the fox on the mainland, and her team's quest, which was roughly analogous to collecting forays made by the fox's namesake, was for data to outline the fox's story. In other words, to answer the question, What is this animal doing here? Six people, one fox.

The gathering of the household in its entirety that evening was a break in the routine caused by Elise's trip out of the park. Early the next morning Elise's small white Ford truck and Christian's white Russian-made SUV headed out with Kate, the two new assistants, Erica, who was on her way to a bus in Angol, and an impressive pile of gear.

After the others drove out of the park, Kelly slung the radio re-ceiver, the device I'd seen the day before, over her shoulder and took up the sheaf of aluminum tubes, which it turned out could be quickly unfolded to look like a small TV antenna. It was midafternoon when we started up the road from the VC. I was hopeful of seeing my first Darwin's that evening, but because I assumed that seeing the foxes was a commonplace in Kelly's work, didn't bother to mention this to her.

Both the research assistant and the radio telemetry equipment are standard features of zoological field research. The presence of assistants allows fieldwork to go on almost continuously while the PI, principal investigator, works elsewhere or perhaps just gets some sleep. Typically research assistants are young people who enlist to learn the ropes, but there are other people who take up the role as a way of life. When one project is completed, they move on to the next. Obviously not all the chores for which assistants sign up involve radio telemetry, but radio tracking is a common, time-consuming task for which helping hands are necessary. It is the usual method of gathering information on animal location. The foxes were collared, and the radio transmitters on the collars would yield data on the foxes' use of land, where they went, when they went there, and which—if any—other foxes went with them.

A half mile up the hill, the road from the VC intersected with the Portones Road, which as its name suggests, led out to the park gate. Here Kelly stopped, unfolded the antenna, twiddled one of the dials on the box on her hip, and raised the hand holding the antenna over her head. "Some people are scanners," she said about radio trackers and swung her arm and the antenna in a sweeping circle above her, "but I am a spinner."

Demonstrating again, she held the raised arm still and twirled slowly in place. Scanning or spinning, the object of the pass with the antenna was to pick up signals emitted by tiny radios the foxes wore on collars around their necks. By getting a fix on the location of the signal, Kelly could record the whereabouts of a fox on that particular day at that particular time. The basic technology, installing a radio on an animal whose movements you want to monitor, can be implemented in a number of ingenious ways. A tiny radio can be inserted under a snake's skin or glued to a bird's feathers, but the collar for mammals has been used the longest.

Not every radio signal would come from a Darwin's fox. There are three species of fox in the park: the Darwin's, or Chiloé (from Chiloé Island); the South American gray fox, or chilla; and the large, leggy fox called the culpeo that often passes through the araucaria preserve.

Elise had trapped and collared fifteen Darwin's, thirteen chilla, and two culpeos, as well as three of the tiny arboreal wild cats called kodkods that had wandered into her traps. The signal on each collar was tuned to a particular frequency.

Kelly spun, and the receiver crackled with static. Drawing a blank, we turned into the road that went toward the park gate. She had a big stride and an unhurried but relentless pace. At a trailhead a couple hundred yards up the road, she paused to spin again. Static. We turned off on the trail that took us out of the old growth and into grassy land stippled with scrub and a few young trees. Kelly stopped frequently and raised the antenna to ask for signals. When, three-quarters of an hour later, a steady beep came through the static, it was exciting, like hooking a fish. Kelly noted the frequency and took a yellow plastic notebook from her backpack to consult a key on the first page. "DF-6," she concluded. "*Dusicyon fulvipes—*"

"—or," I pointed out, "*DF,* Darwin's fox—"

"Right. Number six, the sixth one we collared. This is the at-rest signal. The fox is lying down or sitting still, not traveling at any rate."

Among the rest of her gear in the backpack were a compass and a handheld GPS unit. She found our position with these and noted the facts in the yellow notebook. Then she restowed everything in the pack, folded the antenna, and swung off down the trail again.

Evidently DF-6 was a female because Kelly said, "We need another point, at least one more for this little girl."

Another hundred yards and she spun again. The signal came in reluctantly and much weaker. Kelly worked back and forth over the section of trail we had just walked, trying to find a place where the signal came in as strong as the first reception. A half hour later, she settled on a place and took its readings. By fixing her locations and taking bearings from two points, Kelly was trying to pinpoint the position of the animal at the intersection of two legs of an imaginary triangle. This was a simplified version of the triangulation method that requires three points and locates the fox within a triangle. In either method, the shorter the distance between readings, the shorter the legs of the triangle and the more accurate the estimate of the fox's location. If the fox is moving and the beep that comes through is the activity signal, then the location is dynamic.

"An activity signal sounds just like what you'd expect," Kelly said.

"Real quick—beep, beep, beep—trot, trot, trot. The other beep we might hear—I hope we don't—is long and slow. The mortality signal. Something is wrong with the fox—it's dead or injured and hasn't moved in twenty-four hours. Or the radio is shot."

Daylight drifted out of the park, and by the time we headed back into the araucarias, gloom filled the spaces between the trees. Then quite shortly came true dark. We had covered only part of the route assigned to Kelly's shift and had several more hours ahead of us. During the rest of the shift, I realized, it would be next to impossible to spot a fox or any other animal.

It was too dark to actually see the path, but in some passages it might show up a few yards ahead as a pale strip reflecting light filtered down through the trees. Boulders and downed trees were dark presences on either side of the trail. Sometimes when we stopped and Kelly dialed in the receiver, a little bat would flutter around the tines of the antenna. If the receiver picked up a signal, she would turn slowly. "What do you think? Is that louder now?"

Often we had to retrace our steps and work back and forth to determine where the beep was strongest. Even backtracking, it was difficult to identify the exact spot from which we'd first heard a signal. Kelly's sense of it was surer than mine. As soon as she was satisfied with the strength of the signal, out came a headlamp, the compass, GPS, and yellow notebook.

It was a little after ten when we struck the Portones Road again. The more level footing was a luxury, and Kelly seemed pleased with our four data for the night, the locations for two Darwin's, one chilla, and one kod-kod.

"Do you ever worry about being alone out here at night?"

"I don't work alone at night."

"This isn't night?"

"The night shift is from midnight to seven or eight—when I always have another research assistant with me."

"Dark, then. Do you ever worry about working in the dark with no one else within miles?"

"Well, yeah, you can work yourself up into something like panic if you set it up that way for yourself. You can let yourself think that way about being out in the night, but why psyche yourself out when it's not really dangerous? I was in a lot more danger when I was working in L.A."

"You're alone out here quite a lot."

"I'm equipped for it. I'm good at it, and in fact that was one thing I was looking forward to when I came down here."

The next few evenings of roving the trails of Nahuelbuta gave me time to get to know Kelly, her independence and her habit of thoughtfulness. Heading out in the afternoon with the antenna and the receiver, we talked about Kelly's work, the foxes, conservation work, what she had learned about Chile and Chileans. Coming back to the VC in the dark, we talked about personal things, especially the irreconcilable—men and independence, families and privacy, religion and science.

It was not unusual for Kelly and me to set out from the VC with sheets of rain blowing across the meadow and return in a calm, windless night under a glowing moon. With the Pacific only thirty miles the other side of the cordillera, the weather in the park was seacoast weather with all its sudden shifts. A day that dawned in a heavy drizzling mist might clear by midmorning, and by early afternoon the VC and the meadow might bask in warm sun from a weightless sky.

The park covered fewer than twenty-six square miles and—especially when compared with the campos; logging operations on the ridge; and, down in the Central Valley, the vast acreages of commercial farms—it was a tiny patch of preserve. But we were covering it on foot, and it was easy to forget the Chile outside, the rapid disruption of the Central Valley and the snatch-and-rip logging of the cordillera up from Angol. It was easy to think of the park as a dark-green dominion of old trees that went on forever.

Sometimes it seemed that way. We stayed out until we had hiked the route assigned for the date, and we turned back with as many data as foxes whose locations we had been able to fix. One very good evening we picked up four foxes, and on another rather discouraging night, the only signal the receiver captured was the beep from one of the kod-kods.

Nelson's house would be dark when we returned to headquarters, and in the VC kitchen we groped for matches to light a candle and the propane burner. Dingy is too glorious a word for the interior of the three tiny rooms where the field assistants lived. The place provided shelter and in winter the warmth of the wood stove. Occasionally there was electricity in the VC. In the meadow behind the building, a pipe carried a stream down the mountain to a barn, where there was a turbine, and for some reason everybody referred to the barn itself as the *turbino*. The wheel sent out electricity only intermittently and only for brief intervals. "I never count on it," Kelly advised me about the power. "It can be nice for hot water, but it's usually not good for much of that." She and Jake and Maura seemed oblivious to the darkness and dampness of the rooms and to the impossibility of keeping any surface clean—perhaps because their real quarters were the twenty-six square miles of Nahuelbuta.

At night the temperature dropped dramatically. I put on layers of long underwear and fleece and a headlamp, zipped myself into my mummy bag, and read Darwin's account of the *Beagle* until I was too warm and drowsy to stay with the narrative. I wasn't seeing the foxes named for him, and I wasn't finding any mention in his journal to authenticate the provenance of the species name.

Kelly was unconcerned about our lack of sightings. She was satisfied with the number of radio locations we had fixed, and she offloaded the information from the yellow plastic notebook into a larger spiral-bound notebook that served as the central log of telemetry data. This was kept on a high shelf in the kitchen away from the rice and masa harina, which might have drawn rodents to its pages. Shift after shift on the park trails, and the log filled up very slowly. I was impressed with her patience.

She had a short leave coming up, and she was looking forward to meeting a friend who was flying into Santiago and spending a few days in the city. She could wear clean clothes there and get pizza and pop music. She would leave early on the day Elise and the others were to return to the park. The night before she was to depart, I found what I was looking for in Darwin's journal. The *Beagle* had sailed up from Patagonia to reach the Gulf of Corvado and, in it, Chiloé Island, then called San Pedro Island. The fox innocently presented itself to the crew of the *Beagle*.

> In the evening we reached the island of S. Pedro, where we
> found the *Beagle* at anchor. In doubling the point, two of the

officers landed to take a round of angles with the theodolite. A fox, of a kind said to be peculiar to the island, and very rare in it, and which is an undescribed species, was sitting on the rocks. He was so intently absorbed in watching their manoeuvres, that I was able, by quietly walking up behind, to knock him on the head with my geological hammer. This fox, more curious or more scientific, but less wise, than the generality of his brethren, is now mounted in the museum of the Zoological Society.

No fooling around with radio equipment for him. Darwin hadn't even had to go out of his way to see the fox.

I was as excited to find this as I would have been to come across the fox itself, but the next morning Kelly was so busy trying to pack clothes that were still wet from rains the night before and finish catching up the central data log that I found no opportunity to share my discovery. Her plan was to hike with the leaden pack eight miles out the Portones Road to a tiny settlement just beyond the park gate, Vegas Blancas. Here, at two in the afternoon, she would meet the *micro,* the little bus that ran down the mountain to Angol. Her day was back-timed to the arrival of the *micro* at Vegas Blancas. She had to leave the VC, she declared, no later than noon. Our pace picked up. Clothing, cleaning, transferring data. It became a little frenzied. At eleven-thirty, there was a knock on the door. We called out to come in, and the person who appeared was a tall, bony man in a floppy canvas hat, khaki shorts, and sneakers. We had been too busy to notice his truck pull up beside the Visitors Center.

He introduced himself—Jonathan Losos, an evolutionary biologist from Washington University—and explained that the three men waiting in the truck were graduate students. At the park gate the guardaparque told them there were other scientists in the park. They noticed the pelts hanging behind the turbine barn, he said, and he was just wondering, "What's going on here?"

Good question, and his timing was perfect. Kelly looked out the window, saw the truck, and bolted out of the apartment to ask the students waiting for Losos if they could give her a lift to Angol. This would spare her the eight-mile walk and, an even greater mercy, the ride down the mountain in the *micro.* Losos worked in herpetology. So it was not difficult to explain Elise McMahon's research: the wet paper bags pinned to the clothes line—the scat collection—the soggy fox pelts and the foreleg of a puma hanging on lines behind the turbino, and Kate Doyle's meticulously put up small-mammal carcasses safe and dry inside the barn. The scene and the artifacts of Elise's work were probably familiar to him.

"She's studying the Darwin's fox," I told him. Without an instant's pause, he said, "Oh right. This must be the one he bopped on the head."

I was quite deflated. My new literary find was a discovery to no one but myself, because Darwin is very familiar to anyone who studies wildlife.

Losos and the three graduate students were in the park to collect lizards. Nahuelbuta was one stop on their sweep through all the national parks in Chile, and while Kelly finished packing and transferring data, they drove out into the park. They were surprised when I asked to ride along but were good enough to allow me to wedge myself in the small cab with them. Their snatch-and-grab survey was no more systematic than Darwin's excursions into the interior, but it was a lot more efficient than trying to track foxes. They stopped the truck every few hundred yards at a likely-looking rock or log where the sun shone, and the students scattered out and pounced barehanded on whatever scurried for cover. They zipped the live take in their jacket pockets and climbed back into the truck. The motion of the little truck pitching and rolling on the park road was so violent that it was only when we turned around and headed back to the VC again that I noticed that a small flannel bag hanging from the headrest was jumping with a life of its own—lizards captured in another place the day before.

Kelly was waiting outside the VC, pack at her feet, eager to take my place. "Oh cool," she said about the bag full of lizards and folded herself into the back seat just behind the agitating bag. As the truck disappeared up the road toward the park gate, I sat in the sun with Darwin's journal. Late in the afternoon Nelson Navarro stopped on his way home from park headquarters with a message from Elise. We spoke slowly because his English was only slightly stronger than my Spanish, but we worked out the message: Elise had radioed park headquarters to say she had been delayed and wouldn't be back for several days. I would be on my own until she and her crew returned.

At first this left me feeling oddly dislocated. I was not actually alone, but I would be left very much to myself. Nelson was out in the park during the day, and although, come evening, he was just up the hill with little Vanessa, our difficulty in communicating was a barrier. I was in a forest preserve that I knew hardly at all because my forays into it had taken place in the dark. That night I lay in my sleeping bag as solitary as one of the pumas that lived in the park. But now I unexpectedly had the opportunity to do what I had wished for on Santa Cruz, to walk through the places where the animals lived without a noisy vehicle or the rattle of any kind of equipment.

As soon as the sun struck the tent in the morning, the hummingbirds woke me. They were startlingly large for hummingbirds, about the size of a bluebird, green-brown and speckled like a thrush. The Chileans call them *picaflores*. When they hovered under the lowest branches of the araucaria their wing beats rattled the air. Occasionally one would swoop in and nip the tent. The fabric was red, and evidently the hummers thought my lozenge-shaped shelter was a giant flower. Each day that dawned bright brought them back, helicoptering and diving down to prospect for the sweet spot in the enormous red blossom. The sun stayed with me all week, and I walked out each morning hopeful that my travel would bring me within sight of a fox.

I thought there could be an advantage to being alone in Nahuelbuta. Animals that would flee from two humans with a radio receiver might show themselves to a quieter single presence. To some extent this was true. I saw the big woodpecker called the *carpintero negro*, little brown snakes streaked with silver, and on several occasions when the trail dipped down into dampness, a tarantula the size of a hockey puck. On account of its appealing plumpness and the gold-red fuzz that covers all of it except for the glossy black medallion on its back, the Chileans call this spider *el pollito*, little chicken.

A tiny citron-green frog hopped down in front of my boot toe. Its head was pointed like a dunce's cap. On higher, grassy ground a troop of horses pounded through, driving me off the path. They were the horses the guardaparques rode in winter, when the park roads were too sloppy to be navigated on motorbikes, and they had broken out of their summer pasture on one of the campos.

But I wasn't seeing any foxes, and crossing the rotted-out bridge on the road to Cerro Anay once, I thought enviously of George Schaller and his work on lions in East Africa. His scrupulous observations formed a rich, highly detailed story, almost a novel, of the savanna. His descriptions of lions on a hunt, lions at a kill, raising cubs in cooperation, roaming as single nomads, even lions just sleeping were made possible to a large extent by the setting. The Serengeti was a broad panorama where thousands of animals led their lives in the open. The herding animals—wildebeests, gazelles, zebras—found shelter only in their family groups. The predators—lions, cheetahs, hyenas, and wild dogs—used kopjes, rocks, and occasional trees for cover. Although hunting and kills often took place at night, these and other significant events were also on the animals' daylight agenda. The interactions of the top predator lions with the less aggressive leopard and cheetah, and with the hyena and African hunting dog, could be seen and teased apart relatively easily.

In terms of conservation, an animal's visibility is a strong advantage. It's easier for people to care about and grant property rights to an animal they can see, one that can be readily counted and whose image is easy to capture and publish. But there are many animals, like the population of the Darwin's fox in Nahuelbuta, whose actual survival depends upon invisibility. Out of sight, out of mind. It takes someone like Elise who is willing to spend years to learn the life of the Darwin's and someone as astute, patient, and quick on the trigger as Christian Muñoz-Donoso to photograph it. It was the Darwin's fox's good luck to have settled in a preserve, where seen or unseen, it had the land it needed. But Nahuelbuta's plant life made visibility a matter of feet and yards. I had heard the signals from the radio collars. I knew the foxes were there living in a fox world constructed in the same surroundings I inhabited—the way the coyotes at home shared space without sharing their world—and I stayed alert to the possibility that a Darwin's fox might take a chance or make a mistake and allow the two worlds to glance off each other and itself to be seen. But I walked the trails until the Proyecto Zorro team returned without catching a glimpse of a fox.

As soon as Elise's white truck and Christian's SUV reappeared in Nelson's driveway, both packed beyond capacity with people, gear, and groceries, and Kelly returned from Santiago with her friend Heather, then Proyecto Zorro, Nelson's house, and the VC became a household again: one fox researcher, one small-mammal researcher, three assistants and a friend, one filmmaker, the three Navarros, and me. We commuted back and forth up the path to the Navarros' simple house.

That night was another when everyone was in camp at the same time. I mentioned to the usually silent and attentive Christian the bright green frog I'd seen, and this prompted an enthusiastic exchange. "Darwin's frog," he said when I showed him the pointed shape of its head, "very rare." Through Elise, he told me how lucky I was to have seen it. What I wanted to see was a fox. I could appreciate that the tracking, the triangulation, the accrual of fox locations might generate important information. But even so, I thought that in order to really comprehend the fox or any animal, you had to have an opportunity to observe it. Without this, you would know the fox only the way you know people with whom you only speak on the phone or exchange e-mail but never meet. I assumed that everybody else at the table harbored similar thoughts and that, in part, what had brought us together in Nahuelbuta was the desire to see the fox. Oddly enough, no one else mentioned it.

Jake was contemplating the days on the trail ahead of Maura and him. He asked if the brown-and-silver snakes I had been seeing were venomous. Christian had spent years in Chile's wild places, and Nelson and Elise often deferred to him on matters of Chilean wildlife. Translated by Elise, he assured Jake that there were no venomous snakes in the park. But Nelson said politely that the brown-and-silver snakes were in fact venomous. Christian gave him a doubtful look, and Elise, now translating for Nelson, explained that the snakes had venom but because they were without front fangs to deliver it and relied on teeth in the back of the mouth, the venom was effectively harmless.

That issue laid to rest, the next frightening possibility on the minds of the new assistants was pumas. Nelson shrugged and said, "We don't see them very often," and Christian, whom I knew had spent many nights that summer trying to get a puma in his lens, added, "Not when we want to, at least."

"They don't like to be around humans," Elise said as a matter of fact, not a point of reassurance. "Although Christian did have an experience—Christian, you should tell this."

Through her, Christian said that he and his filmmaking partner were walking back through a preserve on their way home from a day of shooting, and at a stream crossing they saw the puma standing a little ways upstream. It was a cat he knew. He had played with it as a cub in a wildlife rehabilitation facility. "Isn't that weird?" Elise demanded, "that they roughhoused with the animals?" Christian recognized his old buddy and decided it was safe to cross in front of the puma. But the animal hadn't been faring well outside captivity, and he was hungry. If he recognized Christian, it was as a ready opportunity for food, and he leapt on the man. Christian's partner was able to beat off the big cat but not before it slashed Christian in several places. By chance, there was an observation blind a little downstream, and the partner was able to drag Christian into the shelter. They waited through the night. Blood from Christian's wounds drew the puma back to the shelter, and as Christian lapsed into shock, the puma circled the log structure. Occasionally a paw reached under the wall to search the ground just inside the shelter. Finally daylight drew the cat off, and Christian's partner sprinted for help.

Looking up to the expressions around the table, Christian realized how his story must have affected the new field assistants, and he said in English, "A long time ago." Obviously, though, his nearly lethal intimacy with the animal had left him fascinated. He wanted to be able to take another longer look at it and through his video to say something more about it.

Telemetry resumed in earnest. There was no way to avoid working in darkness. According to Elise, the Darwin's fox had been most active during the hours just before dark, just before daybreak, and to a lesser extent, during the night. Maura and Jake each put in several solo telemetry shifts during the daylight to get the hang of the park terrain and the particular antenna and receiver. Then together they took an overnight shift, eleven to seven. They were both fresh from their undergraduate studies, and having never met before they arrived in Chile, they were now sharing space in the tiny bunkroom as well as work on the trail. Both had field experience, and Maura had even done telemetry in a study of moose die-off. During that project she had worked alone in the field, and she was required to follow each mortality signal down to the carcass wearing the radio and to dig out pieces of the liver.

But even with this experience behind her, nightshift in the cordillera was a challenge, and Maura had puma on her mind. Jake was walking ahead of her. There was a noise in the brush alongside the trail—a twig snapping, the husk of a scale from one of the araucarias falling through the understory—something. He paid no attention to the sound, but in the next stride he found himself carrying his new colleague. Like a drowning person who climbs the nearest object in the water, Maura had leapt up and clamped herself to his back. Jake was as frightened as if she had been an actual predator. The two, who to their credit finished out their shift, returned to the assistants' quarters thoroughly rattled.

The next morning I found Elise making cappuccino in a little steam pot on Nelson's wood stove. Evidently the news of Maura's freak-out hadn't reached her yet, and I decided to let that come out how and when Maura wanted it to. Elise hobbled to the window. She was keeping an eye out for Kelly to start off on her shift.

Below us Kelly appeared, leaving the VC with the receiver, and I said, "I find it amazing that you can get people to volunteer for telemetry duty. It's tedium during the day, and working in the dark alone has to take some guts."

"For them," she said, "it's credentials. They're building a résumé."

"But they might never get a good look at a fox."

She shrugged.

"Isn't it frustrating? Doesn't it make you envy Schaller and his lions?"

Elise laughed. "Yeah, *right*. Schaller"—who looms large for all carnivore biologists. "But the pandas were probably pretty tough to get information on."

Everybody else involved with Proyecto Zorro seemed to find the work satisfying enough without actually encountering the animals. During my time in the park I felt there was something amateurish about my desire to see the Darwin's. I kept reminding myself that when Darwin himself was in Chile, he too was an amateur. It was only later after I had been back at the farm for some time that I discovered I wasn't so very far out of sympathy with at least some of the biologists.

George Schaller told me that seeing animals was the most satisfying aspect of his work. And he had seen plenty. His restless inquiries had carried him from eastern Zaire where he had made close observation of mountain gorillas to the Serengeti and its lions. From East Africa he had moved on to Asia to study solitary forest dwellers like tigers and the reclusive panda and then to the elusive animals of the Himalaya, the phantomlike snow leopard and its prey, the enigmatic blue sheep. Sure, he learned how to dart lions and use telemetry in the Serengeti, and, yes, he would continue to adopt emerging technologies such as molecular analysis of DNA "when there is no other way to get the information." But he regarded a field notebook and a pair of binoculars as the only true essentials for studying animals. If he had made any substantial contributions to our understanding of big carnivores and their prey, he said, it was due to the fact that "I like to watch big animals." I was bolstered by this. I like to watch big animals too. Even so, the idea that seeing animals is not sufficient to understanding them was impressed on me while I was in Nahuelbuta.

"You know," Elise responded to my envy of Schaller, "it's not that hard to get a good look at a Darwin's—just go up to Piedra del Aguila [Rock of the Eagle] and sit in the parking lot."

"Yeah." I knew about the foxes in the parking lot, and eventually I would go take a look. But they seemed like corruptions of the real animal to me.

"They're collared," she pointed out. "They're part of the study." She left that fact with me and departed the topic altogether. She wasn't concerned about seeing the foxes. She needed to document which of them was where at what time of day in which season. She was in the park to gather data.

She could afford to be in Nahuelbuta only for a limited time every year, and each datum was slow to come in and therefore expensive. Money pressures aren't unusual for a biologist in the midst of fieldwork for a dissertation, but the budget for Proyecto Zorro was truly lean. During my time in Nahuelbuta and when I visited her, Elise was nearly as preoccupied with money as she was with foxes. She was working on less than twenty thousand dollars a year, and the grant cycle never paused. Even while she was in the field trapping and tracking, deadlines weighed upon her. "I'd like to be able to keep this going another year," she said more than once, and while she didn't speak directly to the financial pressures, her worry surfaced frequently during the day—how much the garage in Temuco had charged her to fix her truck, how much she had to allow for the assistants' stipends, how much for groceries in Angol, for writing paper (for *writing paper!*). "Because," Christian's explanation was translated by Elise, "paper is something you use every day. In Chile the big items you buy once a decade—a washing machine, a television—are pretty cheap. The everyday things are expensive."

In order to get to this point in her career, where she was working in the field and at the same time worrying about money for the next season, Elise had had to work through the drills that confront every graduate student. Scientists have always been trained through an apprenticeship system that is an ongoing demonstration of competence. For contemporary scientists, classroom and seminar performance lead up to the dreaded A exam, which tests the student's grasp of the work that has preceded him or her in all of the fields straddled by the proposed dissertation. I inadvertently telephoned Elise on the morning of her A exam, and when I apologized for intruding at a time when so much was at stake, she said, "That's okay. I'm really not nervous at all. I think I'm ready for this." In Nahuelbuta I brought up the exam again, and she laughed. "I lied. I was in such bad shape I didn't know how nervous I was."

Usually the first part of the apprentice's dissertation embodies a summary demonstration of knowledge of the field. After the research document had been submitted and reviewed by the members of the committee, there is another major career checkpoint, the defense, a rigorous oral examination on the substance of the dissertation. Every fact put forward must be bolstered by earlier authority or new information. The data themselves, their applicability, their statistical implications are subject to intense scrutiny. As Elise was well aware, the standards applied to data and data analysis are as rigorous as those of any scientific journal—or should be—because once the dissertation has been accepted, it will enter the scientific literature as an authoritative source. All of this strikes me as a lonely enterprise, even before the apprentice heads out into the field alone, as Elise did flying down to Chile to study the Darwin's fox.

Ever since Darwin took his geological hammer to the fox on Chiloé Island, it had been assumed in both the New World and Old that the fox occurred only on that island. Partly this was matter of the theory emerging in Darwin's time that island existence isolated a species and its development, and partly it was due to the fact that the Chileans were slow to recognize that some of the foxes around Angol were similar to the foxes that lived on Chiloé Island. Jaime Jiménez, a Chilean biologist who has been monitoring the Chiloé population since the 1970s, says that biological field research is a more recent scientific endeavor in Chile than in the United States, and his research on the island was considered odd. "People thought I was crazy for paying so much attention to the foxes."

The Darwin's foxes on Chiloé Island are tamer, less spooky about humans, and more apt to appear in daylight. Jiménez thinks the reason the foxes on the island are not so shy as the foxes in the park—and possibly the reason Darwin was able to kill his specimen so easily—is that there are no puma on Chiloé. The island, which was inhabited even at the time Darwin stopped off there, is now a resort community built up with vacation cottages. The foxes are known to sneak into these cottages in search of tuna fish cans and other delicacies. They have not learned to be afraid because—except for the implied danger of the vacationers—there are no persistent threats to the foxes. They are the only foxes on the island and the only other carnivores are the kod-kod, the grison (a large killer weasel the Chileans call the *quique*), and the hog-nosed skunk. Like the Channel Island foxes on Santa Cruz until recently, they are top dogs.

In the early 1990s, biologists in the United States began to hear reports from their South American counterparts that rangers in a national park about 375 miles north of Chiloé had reported several sightings of a small gray fox similar to the Darwin's fox. These came at a time when the timber wolf was becoming an icon for the environmental movement, and a number of biologists were keenly interested in how wolves were related to other members of the canid family, the dogs, or more technically, the breadth and depth of the genetic pool in that family. In 1993 a group of up-and-coming biologists, including Todd Fuller and Warren Johnson—members of Elise McMahon's dissertation committee—spent the summer in mainland Chile looking for the Darwin's fox. For weeks they collected only scat. But they went to Nahuelbuta, where the Darwin's takes pains to avoid being seen and, on one of their last days there, noticed a small gray pelt tacked to the wall of one of the campos at the edge of the park. When the scat was analyzed back in the United States, it turned out to be mostly the product of the kod-kod. But the pelt proved the existence of a second population of Darwin's fox, and eventually it drew Elise McMahon, on the advice of Todd Fuller, to Nahuelbuta.

She arrived in Nahuelbuta with a tent, a set of traps, collars, and receiver. She set up the tent not far from where mine was now pitched on the hill behind the VC and lived in it until winter began to set in. Then Nelson Navarro appeared at her campsite with a fresh-baked loaf of bread and an initial invitation to stay with his family. When she left Nahuelbuta that year, Elise had working Spanish, a horse for the project's transportation needs, and—with help from Eric York, a trapping expert sent by Todd Fuller—about thirty foxes trotting under the araucarias in radio collars.

Her second season in the park did not go as smoothly. The trapping got off to a good start, and Elise had two good field assistants. Then she had the accident. The horse was galloping, the cinch broke, and the saddle flew off. Elise went with it. She crashed into one of the numerous boulders that protrude in the roadbed. Her ankle was broken. Three days later, after the tortuous trip down into Angol and a couple of days at a hospital in Temuco, she was on her way back to the States with a botched repair of the ankle that would soon have to be reoperated. The research assistants carried on and were able to get some telemetry data and fecal samples.

Now in her third season in the park, telemetry data on the foxes remained the challenge.

"What's the most important thing you could learn about the foxes in the park?" I asked her.

"How the Darwin's manages in the same territory with the grays, the chillas," she said. "I think that might be the most important theoretical question."

It seemed plausible that the Darwin's foxes had their own system of land tenure, something like our own, and it might be useful to know which owned which and at which time. But I didn't perceive that how "their" land fit with other animals' land, and how the whole of these parts fit with "our" land were critical to the foxes.

Eventually, Elise would publish her findings, as a dissertation and in scientific articles. When her work was recognized by other scientists in animal conservation as authoritative, her assessments of what the animal is and how it is faring would be accepted more or less as fact. The animal's name would be recorded in species accounts, and the scientific community would act in its behalf in dealing with the IUCN–The World Conservation Union and with lawmakers. In roughly the same time that it took Darwin to sail around the world, Elise would have learned the life of the fox named for him and put it on the conservation agenda.

I suppose it was inevitable that, watching Elise's painstaking gathering of evidence, I would become impatient and begin to wonder about this approach to figuring out the animals. I thought, You will have spent three years trying to get round-the-clock data on these foxes and scrambling for the money to do that, and this is the result that would make you and the powers-that-be happy—how these two foxes share this place?

"But then, of course," Elise went on, "there's everything else—diet, home range, breeding arrangements, behavior." All the other answers to, What is this animal doing here? Which could take years to resolve, as other wildlife researchers could testify.

About fifteen years before Elise collared her first fox, a young Scottish graduate student in zoology, David Macdonald, began looking into the lives of red foxes near Oxford. At first he worked without benefit of telemetry. At the time, the British viewed the red fox, which is abundant throughout the British Isles, with the ambivalence people everywhere feel for carnivores. The red fox is a nuisance on the farm, chased round and round in the hunt, trapped and shot as a clever marauder, but also kept as a dooryard pet. This last, intimate aspect of the attitude was reflected by the technology Macdonald relied on at the beginning of his research, the leash. He raised the vixen Niff from a cub and lived with her in his rooms the way many people keep dogs. With Niff on her leash, they went on long rambles. Macdonald allowed Niff to set the course and followed her—often at a dead run. He wanted to learn why she went where she did, what caused her to stop and nose around, and on what basis she chose a place to urinate. He wanted to find out what makes a place a fox place.

When Niff matured, Macdonald brought her a mate and housed the pair in an abandoned tennis court he fenced off. From this mating an extended pack grew, and soon his questions became questions about family dynamics—who called the shots when. But his social experiment blew apart when the tennis court enclosure was vandalized, leaving the foxes free to come and go and leaving Macdonald with only chance as a means to observe them. Not long afterward he was able to put radio collars into play, and he and the graduate students he now had working under him were tracking and mapping the travels of suburban foxes in and around Oxford. The researchers of what they called the Foxlot Project found that the red foxes had established routes and that their foraging between dusk and daylight was guided by habit and pattern. This information may seem trivial, but in scientific circles Macdonald became quite well known for his findings.

"It's no coincidence that the first good behavioral studies had to wait until we had telemetry," John Eisenberg told me. A senior scientist now retired from the University of Florida and directly or indirectly a mentor to a number of scientists I got to know, Eisenberg is an authority on South American mammals. "The radio collar, a safe, injectable sedative, and a good antidote for it—these are what allowed us to follow the animals beyond the line of sight and even to anticipate their movements."

The technology came out of World War II and, like many domestic offshoots of military know-how, made rapid gains in the postwar years by exploiting other defense and space innovations. The early equipment had its limitations. The batteries were very heavy and, compared to those available now, short-lived. But they were suitable for animals like the lions George Schaller tracked so extensively in the Serengeti.

William Cochran, who was working on an ambitious radio-tower system for Barro Colorado Island in Panama at the time this book was written, was one of the engineers who developed the early telemetry equipment. In 1959, when he was a graduate student in engineering at the University of Illinois working on the radio tracking of satellites, he was approached by Rex Lord, a Ph.D. candidate in biology at the university. If Cochran and the people in his lab could build tracking equipment sophisticated enough to receive signals from outer space, Lord wondered, how about tracking signals sent out from a rabbit? Other biologists, he told Cochran, were attempting this with other animals.

The radio Cochran developed for the rabbit operated on a CB frequency, and the report of Lord's innovation at a 1960 meeting of Illinois mammalogists stirred excitement. Bill Cochran's phone began to ring. In the four decades since, he has designed radio transmitters to be worn by animals as different as foxes being tracked from a tower to albatrosses that wore antennas made of fifteen-foot gold wire. The albatrosses were boxed and shipped by navy plane to Wake Island, where they were released, and Cochran tracked their thousand-mile flight to Midway Island. It is in designing equipment to be carried by birds that Cochran has been able to exploit most dramatically the advances in battery miniaturization that hitchhiked on developments in computer memory storage. Even so, he says, the tradeoffs among weight, transmission, range, and battery life remain problematic.

The transmitters worn by the Darwin's foxes and the chillas in Nahuelbuta are a good deal heavier than the ones Cochran designs for birds, and they will usually continue transmitting from one trapping season until the next year's trapping begins. In addition to being fairly long-lasting, the transmitters on the fox collars send the three types of signals Kelly described—at-rest, activity, and mortality—more complex information than transmitters on earlier models. Possible collar failure notwithstanding, radio tracking is a pretty satisfactory stand-in for direct observation, and although Elise complemented her surveillance arsenal with camera traps that captured the images of whatever tripped their motion sensors, the radio collar and receiver remained her primary system for getting a fix on the foxes' habits. Pinpointing animal locations by radio is labor-intensive, and it is very time-consuming. But it is also a remarkably accurate means of location.

This accuracy was dramatically demonstrated to Elise during her second season in Nahuelbuta. "I picked up a mortality signal—the long, slow beep, and I followed the signal to a big gully. At first, it sounded like it was coming from across the gully, but on the other side, I couldn't pick up anything."

She went down to the mouth of the stream that ran through the gully. "It came in pretty strong, and it seemed to be coming from upstream. I tried to bushwhack further up the gully." As she worked her way up into the gully, its narrow walls were steeper, the signal stronger, and the vegetation denser. When the mud and brambles made the ravine impassable, she turned back and went for help from the guardaparques. She and the rangers returned on horseback, tied the horses, and hacked their way to the top end of the ravine. "The signal kept getting stronger. But when we got to the top, it disappeared." The receiver crackled with static.

Elise cast around with the antenna and eventually picked up the mortality beep again, this time from the opposite direction, out the mouth of the gully, and much fainter. The signal she had originally detected had bounced off the back of the ravine and been amplified by its walls. The true signal was the much weaker one, sent over a fairly long distance.

Elise and the guardaparques followed the beep out of the gully and not long afterward came across the carcass of a male Darwin's fox. "He had been shot and just left there. But the collar was missing." No more data from the fox, and no future data from another fox that might carry that radio. "I really needed that collar. They're not cheap, you know, and in order to get another one I'd have to try to order one from the States. Order it and then wait."

The signal from the collar was still beyond them, coming from somewhere out of the park. In Chile all foxes are protected, and the animal had been killed illegally. Because of this fact, the chief guardaparque agreed to ride on with her and try to find the collar. The source of the beep was a campo not far from the park boundary, where no one appeared to be home.

"I went into the yard and was walking around the house with the antenna, and this old woman came out. I don't think she knew what to think. She said she hadn't seen the fox, and she didn't even know what kind of collar I might be talking about.

"I said, 'It's in your house.' I didn't want to scare her, riding up with a state official and all, but I knew the collar was in that campo."

Probably because of the ranger's presence, the woman opened the door and watched skeptically as if Elise, panning around the rooms with the antenna, were witching for water. The beep drew Elise through the house to a shed at the back. To the amazement of the farm woman, the radio collar hung on a peg in the shed. She had no idea how it got there, she protested.

Then her grandson came home. He was a boy about ten. "He said right away that he had taken the collar off the fox, but he hadn't killed the fox—I think he knew that would have been against the law." The collar was the kid's only misdeed, and Elise could see that the radio gizmo attached to it had been too intriguing to resist.

I was beginning to make the connection between data points and the foxes. If all went well, the thousands of locations the field assistants transferred from the yellow field notebooks to the central log would fill in Elise's map of the Darwin fox's activity in the park, through the hours of daylight and dark and the transformations of the seasons.

What usually set the foxes in motion was hunger. Fortunately, the Darwin's fox is not locked into carnivory because it is not a top predator. It is an animal caught in the middle of the eat-and-be-eaten system in Nahuelbuta. The puma's paw is poised over the other mammals in the park—the three foxes, the grison, the kod-kod, the tiny elusive deer called pudú pudú, and even the rats and mice. This is a somewhat richer system of mammals than the one that had existed for years on Santa Cruz—foxes, skunks, mice—and it incorporates what biologists refer to as a carnivore *guild,* two or more predators inhabiting the same territory. I find the terminology amusing: the small and the weak form *communities,* and the powerful and skilled form *guilds.*

The Darwin's fox clings to a fairly low position in the carnivore guild on mainland Chile, and the most common cause of its death, Elise believes, is predation by other carnivores in response to competition for food. Likewise in North America the most common cause of death among wolves is other wolves. Some of the Darwin's foxes that Elise collared and tracked and then found dead were, in fact, puma victims, but a higher number were the work of the two other foxes, the chilla and the culpeo. Whatever the ratios, the presence of three larger carnivores creates enough intimidation to make the Darwin's forage with care, hugging the areas of the park where there is dense growth, while seeking opportunities to pounce and kill. When their luck as predators doesn't hold up or when food is available without the effort of stalking and pouncing, the foxes probably gobble down lizards, birds, bats, insects, grubs, and fruit.

Elise referred to this as "opportunism," without any moral loading, and pointed out a prime example. "I mean, look at the parking lot foxes. Just look at the family in the parking lot."

So I did, finally.

The Piedra del Aguila is an enormous boulder that teeters high on the western face of the cordillera. If you take the log steps propped between the boulder and the even larger chunk of cliff below it, you see the Pacific in front of you, frilly waves reaching up the beach, and behind you to the east, the Andes. In the summer, the Piedra is a sightseeing destination for anyone willing to risk a vehicle on the park roads, and on the nearest patch of level ground, the guardaparques have put up a low log rail to create the parking lot. I hadn't seen anyone else on the path or up on the Piedra, but there was a car parked near the sign forbidding you to feed the foxes. There were no foxes.

I sat down on the rail and shrugged off my backpack to get to my water bottle. At the sound of the zipper, a small fox appeared under the rail on the opposite side of the lot. It looked a lot like the picture of the Channel Islands fox on the postcard. It was only slightly larger than a house cat, salt-and-pepper brindle with bright markings: chestnut starting near its delicate snout and running to short, sharp ears and also covering its paws and lower legs, then a white splash under its chin and a white bib. I didn't move. Neither did the fox. It wore blue ear tags, and a blue antenna poked out from its radio collar. Blue equaled male. This was Papa. I raised the plastic water bottle to drink. He advanced, staring at the backpack. I crinkled a plastic bag inside the pack, and the fox came quite close. When I didn't produce anything, he growled. He and the noise were too small to be taken seriously, though, and after about thirty seconds his threat seemed to make him nervous. He retreated to the very center of the parking lot and sat down to ponder the situation. Finally he ambled over to a sunny spot under the sign forbidding the feeding of foxes, and he lay down. He closed his eyes, appearing to doze, and another fox crept under the rail to recline beside him. With red—for female—ear tags and a red antenna, this had to be Mama. She licked him behind his ear and then closed her eyes too. But they weren't really dozing. They were watching the backpack, waiting to see what it would yield. Mama was much shyer than Papa. Every few minutes he would get to his feet and approach the backpack, but she would follow only a couple of steps and then resume her resting place.

The standoff was broken by a high yip. Mama vanished. A third fox approached from the other end of the parking lot. Blue ear tags, blue antenna—one of their sons. As soon as he took up a post with Papa, identifying himself, Mama materialized again in the sunny spot. Then came the sound of an engine, a car grinding its way up the mountain road toward the parking lot, and the parking lot foxes scattered.

When the visitors, a couple with two young children, emerged from the car, the foxes' routine began all over again. One of the children was a girl about four, and her mother, delighted with Papa, gave the little girl a piece of sandwich. The child held it out to the fox, and the animal growled. She shrieked and clapped her hands, letting the bite of food fall to the dirt. Papa snatched it, and Mama ducked in quickly for the crumbs. Sandwich, fruit, biscuit. All dropped before the fox's muzzle reached the child's hand, all accompanied by coos and squeals. When the family of sightseers turned up the path to Piedra del Aguila on their way to their own picnic, the male fox glanced over at me, walked over to the newly arrived car and lifted his leg against the tire. Then, rechecking some earlier work, he went to the first car that had been left and sprayed the wheel. Clever fox.

Papa and his family were a corrupt bunch. Their strategy was quite efficient—go no farther than the parking lot and food will come to you—but it was also dangerous because it involved humans. How would Papa and his family get their living during the Chilean winter when no one drove up to the Piedra del Aguila? How long, I wondered, could a strategy like this succeed? I hoped that during the misery of heavy snow the parking lot foxes would regain their respectability and do what foxes should do, pounce on other animals and plants and eat them.

I walked back to Nelson Navarro's house wondering if a diet was so diverse, if the fox could make do with just about anything, why bother to research its details when research takes so much time and effort? The work in Nahuelbuta had impressed upon me again the dailiness of field research. It was as relentless as dairy farming, and most of the results were as plain-white predictable. Elise had a pretty good notion what she would end up reporting about the diet of the Darwin's fox. Why spend all this time collecting and picking through fox shit? Why not just say that the Darwin's eats the general run of what an animal of its size and speed might take up from the forest floor, the creek beds and the *turberas,* that is, rodents, insects, and berries?

"Because," Elise said quite patiently, "we haven't determined that." Assumption must wait on fact. The facts are tedious to uncover and perhaps more tedious to observe being uncovered. I could see that if the fox was after enough calories to keep going, Elise was after enough data to do the same: what you need equals the lengths to which you will go to get it.

It was all about data, each datum one atom of observation. Elise's career-making research rides on a stream of minute findings, and the same is true of the larger enterprise of conservation biology. While the purpose of the research may be truly worthy, the researcher's need for information is a personal one. The acquisition of data is the first requirement of any study that will give a scientist a foothold on or another rung up the career ladder. It will affect Elise's—or any scientist's—ability to make a living. This is a fact, a pressure with which any conservation biologist must contend because the Ark floats on a sea of data.

This is the case with any science and has been since the urbane Francis Bacon explained at great length to the court of James I that the only true means of understanding nature was to begin by observing the most minute physical entities capable of being observed, to observe all of nature's tiniest components and to amass these observations until they suggested a statement about themselves, a statement of fact. The statements too would build up and create more general statements. Bacon understood about as much of mathematics as I do, because modern mathematics, never mind the use of data in statistics, had not yet been formulated. Although the absence of mathematics from his argument has subjected the soundness of his logic to periods of historical neglect or outright devaluation, his dogged system of inductive reasoning has become the basis of scientific discovery and its essential skepticism. It is not, of course, without its pitfalls, and Bacon himself regretted that "the [human] understanding is endowed by nature with an evil impulse to jump from particulars to the highest axioms [hypotheses]. . . . This impulse must be held in check; but generalizations lying close to the facts may first be made, then generalizations of a middle sort, and progress thus achieved up the successive rungs of a genuine ladder of the intellect." He exhorted his seventeenth-century readers to undertake this method to observe all of nature and catalog their observations. Bacon evidently prevailed. Although hypothesis—such as Darwin's theory of evolution—usually shortcuts pure induction, this is, more or less, what has been going on since.

While the slow accrual of repetitious fact made me impatient, it was what was expected of Elise and what she expected of herself. Her need for information was the second appetite at work in Nahuelbuta. After a couple of days back at work in the park she had grown quieter and a little watchful. The telemetry hadn't been going smoothly, and the data were coming in only sporadically. The two new assistants were not settling in comfortably. Night work continued to be a problem for Maura. Jake was bored with the telemetry and had made an amicable agreement with Elise to leave as soon as his replacement could be found. Kate Doyle was due to pack up her rodent carcasses and leave the park, and not long after her, Kelly Cruce would go back to the States. Elise had begun to worry about the fact that it was only a matter of weeks before she too would have to leave Nahuelbuta.

What numbers would be written in the yellow plastic notebooks in her absence during the Chilean winter when conditions were harsher and the foxes less active? One black prospect was a big hole in the data, a six-month gap in information. For the young research assistants, it was a volunteer stint, an assignment far from home in a beautiful but hard place that would give them credentials before they themselves resumed their own careers. Sure, the numbers were important, but they would never own the data. Elise was the one who had to do that. She had to have the information.

"Fear" is what David Macdonald told me was going through his mind when he was a graduate student running through English gardens and fields with a young vixen on a leash. Science is a wide realm with a great deal of latitude for failure, and a great deal is left up to the graduate student. For the student it is a lonely test, and there are many reasons to be fearful: You must learn, if not everything, then the essentials of most of the work that has preceded you. For your research, you must not wander too long looking for a topic that can be yours and yours alone. You must have drive and spark but not so much fire you propel yourself into an indefensible scientific scrubland. You must bring in solid, analyzable data. You must do "good science," whether or not you do good for the cause of conservation.

At the outset of his Ph.D. candidacy, Macdonald told me, he had as his goal one that could have been mine, "getting into the animal's skin" in order to be able to "do something practical" for it. But by the time he was running Niff on a leash, these goals had given way to his worries about himself. His advisers at Oxford had all warned him off the study of foxes. They were too difficult. Nobody had been successful in it. Macdonald was extremely bright, and no doubt the dons wanted him as a student, but they wanted him to drop the baggage of fox research. Through what he says was stubbornness, he never veered from his original plan. He had no luck trapping the foxes, but finally, after raising the vixen and coming up with the idea of the leash, he had the possibility of getting some data, some new information. Even at this point, he said, "I was afraid I would fail. In fact, at times I was fairly certain I would fail."

Elise too had a lot at stake, and it rested, like David Macdonald's career, on data she wasn't sure she would get. "What Elise is trying to do is very difficult," Warren Johnson told me. Not only is the animal secretive, but "doing research in a foreign country, even a fairly well-developed country, presents its own set of problems." Johnson, a researcher at the National Cancer Institute well known for his genetic studies of felines, was a member of the committee supervising Elise's dissertation. He told me that after spending a few of his student years trying to do research on the pumas in Chilean Patagonia, he eventually gave up on the animal as a dissertation subject. While he had learned a lot about the big cats, he could not get enough data to support any conclusions. Eventually he turned in a dissertation of comparative research on two common Chilean foxes, the chilla and the culpeo. "It's just not that easy to come up with a good, useful set of data."

To a great extent Elise was at the mercy of the field assistants, and they probably perceived they were at her mercy. Conflicts like this are commonplace in field research. The research assistants work in trying conditions for little or no pay, and their supervisors are often inexperienced managers who are themselves working under pressure and living in close quarters with the assistants under the same conditions. Elise's numbers were in jeopardy. She had been planning to help the field assistants get settled in and leave the park at the end of the month, which was coming up fast. If she stayed in Nahuelbuta, it would be difficult to do what was needed on the home front, write grant applications to get the money to keep Proyecto Zorro going.

Although there was never any outburst, the Proyecto Zorro household silently branched into two camps: the bosses, or the graduate students, up in Nelson's house, and the employees, or the assistants, down in the VC. I suspected Elise was trying to exert more forceful management because Maura and Jake began double-checking the coordination of their rounds and their findings with Kelly, and their trips up to Nelson's house nearly ceased.

The assistants remained quite friendly with me but didn't discuss their situation. Christian Muñoz-Donoso moved comfortably back and forth, a considerate if taciturn emissary. I too was able to float back and forth, although with Maura and Jake more often in residence in the little apartment, I felt less free to impose myself there. I hiked with Kelly and her friend Heather on their shifts, rode in the truck and drank coffee with Elise and Kate, and otherwise kept to my tent.

A few days before I was to leave Nahuelbuta, I wandered up the path to the Navarros' house and into the middle of an intense conversation. Elise was being forced to adapt and was laying out her plans for Kate. She could not leave the park until the telemetry situation was certain. She would advertise the position that Jake would leave vacant. To avoid attracting candidates not suited to the work, she would rewrite the ad to which the current assistants had responded, make it sound tougher. She rehearsed briefly the changes that eventually made their way into the new ad: "Radio-telemetry is done at night as well as in the daytime, there are pumas in the park, it may rain for three weeks straight or snow a meter in a few days, electricity is neither reliable nor consistent, there is no e-mail or other contact with the outside world except for monthly trips into town, assistants work ten hours a day, and to top it all off, the project leader can be very demanding." She would remain with Maura on telemetry until someone willing to accept these conditions arrived and settled in.

Perhaps it would be possible to meet the deadlines for the grants that would support the next year of Proyecto Zorro by working from the computer in her room. She tried to make light of the shift in plans. "I never leave Chile on the schedule I give the airlines," she told me. "I'll just stay as long as I have to." Her immediate need was this year's data.

The data for each day became a stop-motion snapshot of the whereabouts of the two species of foxes and the kod-kods. Taken in sequence, these snapshots would reveal the foxes' daily travel patterns and the size of their home range. These were the most important findings she could come to, and, like those of David Macdonald fifteen years earlier, they were on their face mundane. The story she would take back to the States with her would be a simple story about land and movement, and it would go something like: "There is a fox in Chile. It is rare, only about six hundred in the world. It is small and, for a fox, brightly marked. Its diet consists of . . . It lives in dense, brushy places. It is crepuscular and travels mostly in the hours of dusk and before dawn. In all, each fox needs about seventeen square kilometers for its home range."

The story seemed too spare to be satisfying, and a number of questions about the meaning of this kind of research had started rolling around my head. What was going on in Proyecto Zorro was about facts of fox life, not about intimate observation of an animal in its natural scene. It didn't really matter whether I saw a fox or how often Elise saw a fox. What mattered were the data.

Kelly and I went out in the afternoon after a rain. Elise was confined with her data in her room at Nelson's. Kate Doyle was checking the traps she set for small mammals, and Christian was lurching over the park roads in search of the optimum camera position from which to shoot the moonrise when the weather cleared. Dense clouds clung to the mountains, which were greener in this gloom. Sunlight emphasized the gray in the araucaria trunks, the Spanish moss, and the rocks. We walked uphill for a couple of hours, scanning every few hundred yards for beeps, and this long effort yielded one location for Kelly's notebook. She had passed months with this kind of productivity.

We found dry ground and some large boulders to seat us for lunch. "This business of locating beeps hardly seems fair," I said, not able to resist dragging the hammer story out again. "All Darwin had to do was walk up behind the fox on Chiloé."

"No kidding," Kelly accepted the information in the story pleasantly. "A hammer?"

We drank our water and decided to unwrap the peanut butter sandwiches.

"How often do you actually see a fox?" I asked.

"Not very. Not very often at all. In fact, I'd say it's rare."

We tucked away the sandwich wrappings and followed the road's twin ruts into dense growth, where it was now dark. "Visuals," Kelly came back to my question, "actual sightings, aren't that important." She meant important to the telemetry process, but actually laying eyes on the foxes still seemed very important to me.

We had nearly finished the shift when we came to the Portones corner a few hundred yards from the VC. Kelly spun slowly with the antenna, casting for fox activity. Immediately a beep sounded. A female at rest, Kelly decided, and she began fixing the location. I'd watched it all before, and the reckoning of compass points was no longer arresting. I wasn't following the antenna but looking back in the direction from which we had just come. There was, unmistakably, a fox in the road, and the fox was trotting toward us purposefully, as if he had an appointment.

Under my breath I said, "Kelly!"

She was fooling with a knob on the receiver.

"Kelly!" I hissed, and that drew no response. Unbelievably, the fox was still coming on. I backed up and jabbed her in the side. "Look!"

The fox came to a halt to consider us. It was gray, a little taller than the red foxes I saw often at home. Like the red foxes, this fox showed no concern about being caught in the sight of humans: Look if you like, don't look if you don't like. I have other, more pressing business. The fox resumed travel, coming slightly closer, then making a neat corner into scrub growth as if that had been his plan all along.

Kelly laughed. "It's one the chillas, the husband of the female who was just checking in."

"How do you know?"

"Didn't you see the collar and the blue ear tags?"

I hadn't. I had been too taken with the sight of the fox.

"They hang around this corner a lot, and they get to know all the assistants by name. He probably went home and said to his wife, 'Have you seen the new one with Kelly?'"

"How come we didn't pick up his signal with the receiver?"

"He came up behind us."

5 ⁓ Loners

IT WAS HIGH SUMMER IN CHILE, AND THERE SHOULD HAVE been fox pups in the park. By this time of year any young should have started to travel and forage on their own. But Parking Lot Mama and Papa, whose food supply gave them a much easier berth than foxes in other parts of the park, apparently had no new kits this season, and no one in the park, including the guardaparques, had seen any other pups. The number and health of young are a good indicator of the vitality of a wild species and, for an animal as rare as the Darwin's fox, an important one. So I wondered what the absence of kits meant.

With the beeps of radio collars flitting about like so many fireflies and only sporadically coming within range of the assistants' receivers, I found it hard to imagine more than one radio collar, more than one fox in the same place at the same time. Obviously, males and females had to meet up, and kits had to be nursed and supervised and weaned. But the dark shade under the araucarias and dense undergrowth in the more sunlit areas of the park seemed an impenetrable curtain for fox encounters and family intimacies. These events would seem to take place off stage. They were mysterious to me, as I think they are to any scientist studying an unknown animal.

The social life of an animal is a complex set of phenomena, and it is often the last piece of the animal's natural history to fall slowly into place. This takes a long time because in animal societies, including our own, not every relationship, every interaction, is what it appears to be. If I see a man and a woman walking together, what should I assume about their relationship? If I know two animals travel the same route in close succession, the question about their relationship is far more complicated to answer.

"The main reason why so many species are considered solitary," carnivore biologist Paul Leyhausen has observed, "is that they can only be shot one at a time." It takes something more ingenious than a gun to come up with the facts of sociality. Our observations are limited by the fact that our senses do not synchronize with animal senses. Right now we have to rely heavily on tools based on logic and deduction: telemetry, a stand-in for sight; behavior studies of captive animals; and genetic analyses of scat and hair and blood. These still leave us with a significant burden of long-held assumptions, many of them mistaken, about who is what to whom. We've always known and acknowledged that about people—it is one of the bases of great literature—and my experience in Nahuelbuta was evidence of how easy it is to become comfortable with your own assumptions about social relations. But because reproductive success and survival hinge on social life, it's important to establish who is what to whom.

I went out with Elise and Christian to set and rebait camera traps. Elise's ankle was healing, but she was still quite lame, and hiking for any significant distance could cause the pain to tune up. Christian drove, and his capable vehicle ground down into the hollows around the boulders and wallowed up and out, only to sink down into the next. At points marked by surveyor's tape tied on tree branches, he stopped, and Elise got out to check the bait and the film supply in the camera.

"Does it worry you that nobody is seeing any signs of pups?" I asked.

"Well," she equivocated, "a little maybe. But we haven't really started trapping yet this year. And these camera traps may get some photos."

"Is it possible there are none?"

"Sure," she agreed, "a lot of things are possible."

"Why would it be that the foxes have no pups?"

"Any number of things—disease, predation, or maybe they're facing some other kind of reproductive threat." Elise was not leaping over an absence of data to any conclusion. The lack of sightings was not evidence of a lack of cubs.

I had my own theory. "Do you think it could be the ear tags and the radio collars?"

Elise looked baffled. "I'm not sure what you mean."

"They're wearing a lot of big jewelry for a little animal. Do you think it could be getting in their way?"

"You mean when the foxes mate? That's pretty unlikely."

When I suggested this theory to Roland months later, he gave me his museum docent response—a sure sign I am heading off the path of science into amateur's underbrush. He was level and respectful, as if he were seriously considering the possibility that the collars and ear tags could have shut down the reproduction of a rare Chilean fox, and he said, "I know of nothing in the literature that suggests radio collars could produce that kind of problem." But I was concerned about what I silently referred to as "tinkering," about scientific intervention in nature. Hadn't Werner Heisenberg's questions about the effects of scientific observation on its subject—in his case, subatomic particles—proved that the process of observing necessitated manipulation of the subject and its possible alteration?

It seemed perfectly logical to me that the ear tags—which looked large and heavy on the small, thin shells of their ears—could be inhibiting the foxes' mating. If foxes and other canids were wary enough of human gizmos carrying human scent to make trapping them a challenge, why wouldn't they suspect the manmade collars and tags loaded with pungent evidence of human handling?

Perhaps something of the situation would be revealed by the end of the Chilean summer after Eric York had worked his magic with the traps, the camera trap film had finally been developed back in the States, and Elise's tracking data showed the activity patterns for the foxes. Also, Elise had been collecting blood samples, and the DNA assays of these could reveal a lot. Not by themselves, Warren Johnson cautioned me. "How much Elise's DNA samples will tell us depends on how good her field data on the individual animals are—her telemetry locations, the information from the camera traps." In other words, to know that DF3 and DF14 are mates is to know very little unless you know where DF3 and DF14 go and when they go there. PCR and other molecular techniques cannot answer every riddle in natural history.

Fortunately Elise did not set out to create a detailed description of the Darwin's social life, because for this she would have had to stay in Nahuelbuta until she was an old woman. But since she had made the decision to stay on in Nahuelbuta long enough to keep the telemetry data coming in until a new assistant arrived, tensions between the two factions of Proyecto Zorro seemed to dissipate. Jake spoke openly of his return to the States and the reunion with his girlfriend. Maura had begun to pursue with Elise the idea that her boyfriend might be the one to take Jake's place, and Elise was pressed hard enough for help that she was considering this. Both assistants were clear in their intentions to mate, and it would have been far more convenient for Proyecto Zorro if the foxes had been equally clear about theirs. The assistants went out with their receivers, and late in the afternoons Christian ferried Elise around the park to the camera trap sites.

Down in the VC I overheard Maura and Jake referring to Elise and Christian as if they were a couple or at least romantically involved. It seemed a possibility, but a remote one. I never saw them touch, never mind kiss or cuddle, and I had never caught them exchanging the private glances that lovers do. They seemed no more attached than Maura and Jake, who had met just a couple of weeks earlier but were now occupying the lower and upper bunks in the grim little apartment. We were all having to share the limited space in the VC and Nelson's house.

It seemed to me that Christian was in Nahuelbuta for his videography of the foxes, which occupied the hours of darkness, and during daylight he was being a nice guy, helping out with the driving so that Elise, who was hindered by the injured ankle, could keep up with her research. Was I too far beyond breeding age myself to recognize a mated pair when I saw one? I didn't think I was that blind. Maura and Jake were at an age when people mated as readily and haphazardly as pool balls ricocheting off each other. Maybe to them Elise and Kate seemed like loners and somewhat incomprehensible in their commitment to their work and willingness to undertake it independently. Maybe it was easier for the assistants to understand Elise and Kate if they could assign some sexual agenda to them.

I myself did not intend to poke around in Elise's personal life. The foxes were my interest, and I respected her independence. She would let me know what she wanted me to know, and certain things did come out. She and Kate spoke with me a number of times about men, problems in the balance of power between men and women, and the shortage of acceptable men. There were very few really good men to start with, the two of them agreed, and by the time you reached your thirties and were still struggling for professional standing? "*None,*" Kate pronounced. I think she found this particularly hard because she had her son to think about, a precious pup to protect. Christian, characteristically silent, listened quite comfortably to their assessments of his gender.

I assumed he was a disinterested listener and offered some rude advice. "You need to expand your hunting territory." Easy for me to say. I had bumped into a good man during my own time of ricochet. I said, "You don't have to hook up with another scientist or even an academic. There are lots of other kinds of men."

Kate gave me a long, dubious look. "It's hard to know how to meet the other ones," she concluded, "or even to know if I want to."

But Elise said, "I know," with an agreeable little smile. I assumed she was a loner, a person who could be alone and be okay. A career in science, in spite of its opportunities for collaboration, demands self-sufficiency, and for this Elise was well equipped. The only problem with this capacity for solitude—one I am often aware of in my own solitary line of work—is that it has a sinister tendency to expand. If you exercise the aptitude for being alone, it grows stronger.

Kate and Elise's situations might have been of personal interest to me. But at this point in evolutionary history, the matings of particular humans, as impervious to understanding as they are, have little importance. For the evolutionary moment, we humans have success. But most wild animals are still working out their futures, and that is why it is so important to understand their breeding and kinship arrangements and to have some idea of how much and what kind of space these arrangements require.

Mating and reproduction are land-use issues, and the foxes' use of Nahuelbuta was largely directed by scent. When Elise had finished compiling the telemetry data from Proyecto Zorro, she would have a map of where the foxes go, when they are likely to be out, and which foxes travel in proximity to each other. Her map, however, would be only the crudest approximation of the maps the foxes create through the information they receive through their nostrils. Their world, and the world of carnivores in general, is olfactory. Their sense of smell dominates their other senses. In comparison, our capacity to detect odors is shriveled and pathetic. To them odor is the most important information. To us, it is incidental.

While the Nahuelbuta foxes do not seem to travel together often or to come face to face under the araucarias, they have an acute sense of who is in the neighborhood, which foxes and which other animals came and went and how long ago. They know how to keep their distances from other foxes and other carnivores because each fox marks his territory and his travels out of that area, chiefly by spraying urine on landmarks. Each posting can give the next fox who passes through the area important information about its author: the gender and possibly the age, how dominant it is, whether or not a female author is in season, how long ago the urine was applied and, by scent formulas about time and distance, how far away the author might be. Feces carry a good bit of fox gossip as well, and it is possible that the odors given off by scent glands under the tail, on either side of the anus, and between their toes provide further details. The markings and leavings of other kinds of animals also alert the fox to the possibility of becoming prey.

The Darwin's fox, like many other carnivores, lives both a solitary and a social life, and scent is the primary mechanism that smooths the transitions from solitary travel to social activity. The reintegrating power of scent has been easy to observe in the carnivores that pack up—the wolves, African hunting dogs, and hyenas. Although on the surface their family lives may look like cozy, good-natured arrangements—pack mates helping with the hunt and aunts and uncles pup-sitting—there is significant tension in the power structures of the packs. There is the potential for any dominant-subordinate relationship to violently reverse and ignite other volatile relationships throughout the pack. Clans of spotted hyenas are so intensely social that they carry out almost every life function, including defecation, in groups. But they are also prone to bickering and occasionally to lethal fights, after which the winners eat the losers. Usually, though, the hyena's ritual greeting, reciprocal presentation of the anal glands, maintains order by reestablishing bonds between individuals throughout the clan.

In contrast to the hyenas, the Darwin's foxes may seem almost asocial, but still scent plays a cohesive role. This is especially true when it comes to mating. The lifestyle of a solitary carnivore predator is, as R. F. Ewer points out, an obstacle to the possibility of sex. The carnivore competes with its own kind for food and, to get enough food, travels over relatively large territory. "It may take longer for male and female to locate each other and still longer before they can come together and permit physical contact with a partner who may have been previously unknown or even hostile. Since carnivores are well armed these preliminaries cannot be hurried and in most species, the female's oestrous period is long." So it is with the male and female Darwin's fox traveling different hillsides in Nahuelbuta. But somehow, sometime, the loners have to make a dramatic break from their solitude.

So far as I know, there has not yet been a documented observation of the mating of a Darwin's fox. It is unlikely the assistants will ever pick up on their receivers an act of sex between foxes. Furthermore, while the observation of these acts might add some glittering detail to Elise's species account and my own story, it would probably not add much of significance to what is already known about fox matings or carnivore copulation in general—which is plenty. Enough for me to infer how this is likely to happen between Darwin's foxes and to put this scenario into the perspective of the many arrangements that have evolved among carnivores to get the mating job done.

It is not automatic between the two solitary travelers. Timing is critical. If the male wanders up to a female and she is not truly receptive, he may be treated to a snarling demonstration of bitchery. If the dog fox allows the ripe moment to pass without checking in, another male fox may jump on the opportunity. If he intends to cover more than one vixen, each of whom will have established territory of her own, his forays will be many or quite possibly just lengthy. These challenges are compounded by the fact that all the females tend to come in season about the same time, and it's easy to imagine breeding season in Nahuelbuta as hectic and haphazard with mostly solitary foxes bumbling into encounters that often as not turn inexplicably violent. Again, scent is the social mediator.

If it takes carnivores a long time to come together, it takes them a comparably long time to come apart. Ferrets have been observed to copulate for three hours or more, and wolves for two hours. Like the males of other animals in the dog family, the male Darwin's fox has a physical mechanism that prevents him from uncoupling for as long as ten minutes after he makes what dog breeders refer to as "the tie." Near the end of the penis is a gland, the *bulbus glandis,* and when the male has penetrated and ejaculated, the gland becomes engorged and makes it impossible for the male to withdraw. This results in the helpless, hilarious pose that anyone who has seen dogs mate will call to mind immediately. The two animals stand side by side or facing in opposite directions, wanting nothing to do with one another, just waiting out the ludicrous organ that locks them together.

In most carnivores—the dogs, the cats, weasels, mongooses, raccoons—all in fact but the hyena, this organ has an interesting arrangement. It has a skeleton, a shaft of bone called the *baculum,* the *os penis.* This is the black-cat bone, the talisman of machismo mentioned so often in the blues. It varies intriguingly in size and shape across the different species, and in the late 1940s a French zoologist carried out a series of researches, "études systematiques de l'os pénien," that described the baculum in all the carnivore families. In the tiger it is a short, crude blade only about a half inch long. Having never actually laid eyes on a black-cat bone, I can only extrapolate from the size of the tiger's *os* the reason a black-cat bone is carried in a pouch hung around a man's neck: it is so that, like a tiny precious piece of grain, it can be located when the need arises. The fox *os* and the coyote *os* are longer, more refined rapiers, and the bacula of males in the weasel family are graceful hooks. To this hook, the kinkajou's *os,* which is nearly three inches long, adds a fanciful fork at the business end.

The purpose of the *os* has never been agreed upon, although a number of evolutionary explanations have been proposed. In many carnivores, the female is quite a bit smaller than the male, and some scientists think the baculum functions as an insertion guide to overcome the difficulties presented by the differences in size. This theory, however, would not account for the very long, ornate bacula of the kinkajou and the raccoon, where the males and females are about equal in size. Other biologists have pointed out that for a good number of carnivores ovulation does not occur spontaneously with the onset of estrus. Females of these species must be stimulated by copulation before their ovaries release eggs. The baculum could be a prod to stir this activity. There has been relatively little opportunity to test this theory because spontaneous ovulation or the lack of it has not been established in many species. For animals like the Darwin's fox and the coyote that spend a good deal of time in solitude, however, the need to induce ovulation would seem to have the advantage of not wasting eggs when there are no sperm for miles.

The mating is straightforward compared to the families it produces, and this is even more true of animals than it is of humans. If the novelists who concentrate on the intricacies of human families were to shift their focus to animals, their fictional possibilities would expand by an order of magnitude. The neat little sets that humans seem to find so comfortable and often impose on domesticated animals do not carry over into the natural world. There, animals make the most of the resources at hand—food, water, cover—and these arrangements are referred to by biologists as reproductive "strategies," as if they were conscious plans instead of reactions to need and opportunity. The result is a diversity in the structure and size of animal families that has stretched some powerful imaginations. Darwin was amazed when, in his systematic study of barnacles, he discovered sexual mates in a barnacle species assumed to be hermaphroditic: "The male," he wrote to J. S. Henslow, "or sometimes, two males, at the instant they cease being locomotive larvae become parasitic in the sac of the female, & thus fixed & half embedded in the flesh of their wives, they pass their whole lives & can never move again."

Among mammals in the carnivore family there are also some startling arrangements—like the male stoat that impregnates his infant daughters in a reproductive race against high mortality—and many different manifestations of the roles of male, female and of mother, father. The female spotted hyena is markedly larger than the male and with a clitoris that becomes erect like a penis—but only for social and not sexual encounters. She is dominant, her cubs are born well developed, and she often leaves them in a communal underground den. In this chamber they are safe from the predators that include the male hyenas with whom she cooperates to defend territory.

Among canids like the Darwin's, a family in which a number of females gather with a lead male is not at all unusual. In wolf and African hunting dog packs, only one female mates, and the others— her sisters or daughters—put off any blessed events in favor of helping raise the young dogs produced by the head female until that dog dies or loses her breeding viability. It's not so very different from the arrangements of honeybees, and in almost every order of animals there are examples of what used to be called altruism and is now referred to as cooperative breeding, families in which some members of the family deny their own breeding prospects in order to support the nurturing of offspring from another member of the family.

The colorful diversity of breeding arrangements throughout the carnivore order is expressed in the dog family as flexibility. David Macdonald and his colleagues believe that canids are unusually willing to bend their breeding habits and family structure to accommodate to food availability and territory size. The coyote's behavior, for example, changes with the landscape and the population density. Where times are good, territory is not shared, and humans are scarce, the coyotes will form packs, not so large and intensely cohesive as wolf packs— where both the males and the females form hierarchies—but nevertheless packs, in which only one female mates and is "settled." Where coyotes are few and far between, usually because they are hunted or poisoned by humans or where the territory is broken up, the animals go it alone. The dog and the bitch form a seasonal mating pair, which may or may not form again the following year, and the pups mature to scatter out on their own.

Two different populations of the same dog species in two different places may well take different approaches to mating and rearing pups. Some foxes in some places are solitary foragers who at certain times of the year commute back and forth to a cozy den occupied by a spouse and a few pups, while a few species like the arctic fox live in larger packlike groups of a single male and several females. Coyotes with larger unfractured territories and sufficient food will pack up and apparently raise pups communally.

Our understanding of the social and sexual complexities in species we view as far below our own is usually incomplete. Male red foxes, for instance, have been generally credited as being monogamous. This assumption is probably about as accurate as the assumption about animal solitude: we assume that what we see of an animal is what there is to be seen. When we saw a particular male keeping company with a particular female over a breeding season, we assumed that that vixen was the only one with whom he mated. Although we weren't able to see beyond this pair going steady year after year, it is now clear that in certain places where the red fox lives, the male foxes sneak off to mate with other females. In some locations in Great Britain, red foxes actually pack up.

The chastity and nonchastity of foxes and the identification of the cuckolds among them are not merely biologists' gossip. They are important conservation issues. Reproductive strategies are really ways of doing animal business that maximize their chances—or really their genes' chances—of surviving. For altruists like the female African hunting dog who puts off bearing her own pups and the workers in a honeybee hive, there is no payoff in the form of direct descendents. What is their reward for cooperation? Their genes are carried on in the genetic constitution of the pack or hive.

The questions that led to this idea about the real goals of breeding were brought into scientific discussion by a number of biologists studying social insects and birds, most prominently William Hamilton Jr. The conundrums that breeding behaviors presented were later resolved through the use of game theory. This is a widely used mathematical approach that blossomed from essentially one philosophical puzzle about motivation. The Prisoner's Dilemma is a problem in logic that addresses the questions, Why cooperate? And when?

A great number of logical proofs were devoted to resolving the dilemma as it concerns animals' breeding arrangements, and there was even a global contest, organized by Robert Axelrod, a political scientist at the University of Chicago, aimed at optimizing the resolution of the puzzle. The upshot was that any breeding behavior, including the most remote variation on male + female = babies could be explained as the route to maximizing the replication of the individual's genes. I have no idea how a game theorist would plot the scenarios of the philandering male red fox and resolve its genetic rationale, but it is obvious that mating with females unrelated to his usual consort maximizes the influence of his genes.

Obviously, this approach to understanding animal procreation addresses only the behavior and its results. It says nothing about how the behavior came to be. It says nothing about the trial and error through which some animals reproduce successfully and others disappear to failure. It says nothing about animal learning. If Parking Lot Mama and Parking Lot Papa have no cubs one year, or if their cubs do not survive, will they change something about the way they are living? Or will their combinations of genes simply become one that is not carried forward in the Darwin's fox?

Elise and I didn't talk any further about the question of fox pups. She was facing an article deadline and Kate's departure for the States, which because of the need to tote specimens would involve painstaking preparations. When I left the park I made a note to follow up with Elise as soon as she had had a chance to go over the evidence. Before I could learn the outcome of her season in Nahuelbuta, I spoke with

Bill Cochran about the development of telemetry. I tried to ask him if it was possible that the collars and antennas, which he had had a big part in developing, could be interfering with the mating of the foxes. But I had to wait to finish my question until he stopped laughing.

"No male—when he gets ready—is going to let a little thing like an antenna get in his way," Cochran hooted. "He's just going to go for it!"

He was right, as it turned out. When Elise developed the photos taken by the camera traps, there were cubs in them, and later young-of-the-year turned up in the traps Eric York helped her set. "Everybody is very fat," she reported with great satisfaction, as if she had had a part in raising the kits.

When the holidays came, they brought a Christmas card featuring a snug bungalow in deep snow. Warmest wishes from Elise and Christian.

6 ⧤ The Uses of the Dead

THE DAY WAS BRIGHT, THE ACUTE SUNSHINE PROMISING TO stay that way, and as I sat on the grass in front of the turbino, I was nearly overcome by a powerful, putrid stench. Partly it was the odor of a chemical like formaldehyde or formalin, but mostly it was the smell of dead animals. I hadn't anticipated the importance of animal corpses. But, starting with the coyote carcasses packed in party ice, then roadkill deer, and now Kate Doyle's research specimens, my travels had led me from one dead animal to another.

Kate's mission in Nahuelbuta that summer was a census of the "community" of small mammals that likely were prime prey for the foxes, and the *ratas, ratones, ratoncitos, lauchas,* and *lauchitas* she had trapped and killed were stacked up, gutted and preserved impeccably with tiny labels strung around their legs with thread, in clear plastic boxes.

The floor of the araucaria forest is a continuous, intricate patchwork of microterrains that run in and out of the deep shade under the trees. The damp, stony ground there, with its bamboo, mosses, and ferns, drops down to the borders where the great trees mix briefly with wild fuchsia, lantana, and bougainvillea before opening out to grassy hillsides studded with little boulders. Rodent territory, all of it, but some of the neighborhoods are more particular to certain *ratas* and *ratones* than to others. She had been trapping and preserving at a rate Darwin himself would have approved—and I imagine that at the same time he would have envied her taxidermy skills.

The variety of small stuff was impressive. Of the 950 species of mammals in South America, 72 percent of them are bats and rats. According to John Eisenberg, there are still many species about which nothing is known except their name and many more still to be identified. These are not such glamorous subjects as the puma and the

Darwin's fox, and what we have managed to learn about them has often been due to their roles in human disease. "There's been a lot of good natural history done on the back of the public health service," Eisenberg told me about the state of rats-and-bats knowledge. The great number of rodent species may in part be responsible for the trend toward studying them as communities.

When I first saw her specimens, I assumed that she had caught them in snap traps like the mousetraps you buy in the supermarket— which in fact was sometimes the case—and I marveled at the perfection of the pelts and skeletons. "Well, often—when I catch them in box traps—" Kate advised me with a very direct gaze, "I do have to kill them."

"Oh, right," I said, even though this was the first time I had encountered this necessity. "Sure." But it struck me that at least in her line of research we were still in the nineteenth century, not far from Darwin and his hammer.

"I don't like it. In fact, I really don't like it," she said. "I have a way of doing it so that there is very little stress on the animal," and she showed me how she turned a mouse on its back in her palm and used both thumbs to apply firm, deadly pressure to the sternum. I winced.

It was poise, I imagined, that allowed Kate to complete the procedure. A person has to get what she needs. She was a scientist. A scientist needs data. I was beginning to entertain the notion that the foraging equation—what you need equals how far you will go to get it—applied as much to the biologists as to the animals they were studying.

I was rather in awe of Kate. She was cool-headed and self-possessed, focused on her work in the park and her young son back in Amherst. She was working with only a master's degree but had come fairly far in a scientific career because she was an expert taxidermist. Kate was slim and had pale, translucent skin with definite freckles. Unlike the rest of us, she always seemed to have clean clothes. Her long fall of auburn hair was always shiny, and most remarkable, I thought, for someone who handled so many dead animals, her nails were pristine. She was an unlikely-looking executioner, but she had no use for live specimens.

"Probably," I suggested hopefully, "you would rather catch these critters in the snap traps."

"No," she said. "Snap traps can be useful, but they tend to smash up the animal. Things hemorrhage. It's hard to get a good representative specimen."

"So then," working my way to the realization, "you had to kill all of these animals." I was thinking of the young Darwin out hunting in the English countryside to get some of his earliest data, blasting away with birdshot and taking great interest in the final tally of dead birds.

"Not all of them." She took my comment literally.

The information each small carcass had to offer Elise, other than establishing its own identity, was mostly in the hairs in its pelage and its skeleton. She could match these up with bits of the same kind of animal item she sifted from the fox feces. This would indicate what the fox liked to catch or just what it could catch. The range and number of the small mammal species whose parts turned up in the feces at particular times of year would indicate something about the flexibility of the meat component of the fox's diet.

I spent most of the day helping her make an inventory of her specimens for the customs officers in Santiago and for her own use at the University of Massachusetts museum.

Kate failed to notice the stink. She held up the fur shells of *ratas*, *ratones*, and *ratoncitos* stuffed with cotton and the clear jars swimming with organs, and she read out the numbers written on tags tied with thread to the animals' spindly limbs. I recorded the numbers in yet another yellow plastic notebook and breathed through my mouth to stave off nausea.

Although blood and trauma didn't intimidate me, an animal that was actually dead made me decidedly uneasy. I never got used to looking at the dead ones. While I did get better at it, I could not share the intense interest of Elise or Roland. They knew the purposes of animal remains, and they had plans for their dead things.

Behind the turbino, strung from one corner of the barn across its L, was a clothesline. Drying on it were the front limb of a puma dismembered by an unknown agent and the ratty pelt of a Darwin's fox that had died of natural causes. Only a few such pelts have been collected for scientific purposes. The first came from the fox that Darwin coldcocked on Chiloé Island and is now in the archives of the dead at the London Zoological Society. Another pelt went home with the entourage of American scientists that came down to Chile in 1993 to investigate reports of the Darwin's fox on the mainland. Elise was understandably protective of her pelt and the puma paw drying beside it, and she kept a close watch on any visitors who might offer to stray beyond the VC toward the turbino. While Elise made the rounds of her camera traps and input the data from the radio collars, the fox pelt hung there unattended, like the identity of its owner.

The reason that Elise and other biologists keep dead animals around is that dead animals hold still to be examined. The usual reason to look at animal remains is to determine the animal's identity, what that animal is in relation to other animals, how it is like or unlike similar animals. The often theoretical and contentious practice of zoological classification reduces the central question of an animal's natural history—What is this animal doing here?—to an even simpler but more mysterious question, What *is* this animal? And the answer to that question can affect whether or not the animal is put on the conservation agenda and often whether the animal is allowed to keep its hold on the place it lives or onto some land somewhere. At the time I was in Chile, I considered the issue of classification about as appealing as dust, and I was helping Kate with her recordkeeping only to make her departure from Nahuelbuta easier. I didn't recognize what I do now, that there are links between identity, land, and conservation. They may not be direct, but they are present and vital.

Classification is the engine that has driven scientific understanding of biological processes. From its earliest practice by the Greeks and until the mid-nineteenth century, biology was preoccupied, overwhelmed in fact, by the chore of classification. Like Adam, zoologists had as a first assignment the naming of the animals. It was the urgency of the duty to classify that led to a famous rift between two nineteenth-century French biologists. In Paris in 1830, Frédéric-George Cuvier and Étienne Geoffroy Saint-Hilaire engaged in a series of acrimonious debates that caused a furor in intellectual circles throughout the Continent. These battles prompted Goethe, an ardent amateur naturalist, to exclaim, "The volcano has come to an eruption; everything is in flames and we no longer have a transaction behind closed doors. . . . I am speaking of the contest, of the highest importance for science, between Cuvier and Geoffroy Saint-Hilaire, which has come to an open rupture in the Academy."

At issue was the true basis of scientific classification. Cuvier, the more established and imperious of the scientists, was the author of a manual carried by Darwin on the *Beagle*. It was his belief that animals should be classified according to variation in the functions of their parts. Geoffroy Saint-Hilaire had vigorously proposed a theory that presaged Lamarck's ideas about inherited adaptation and would organize the animals according to the progression of variation in their structures. This difference in philosophies caused the two biologists to assign animals to wildly different categories and to cripple the progress of classification—and of French biology—until the issues were resolved.

Six years after the Cuvier–Saint-Hilaire debates, Darwin returned to England on the *Beagle*. Although within a few years he would become preoccupied with questions about species—what they are and how they are created—at the time he brought out the specimens he had collected from the *Beagle*'s hold, he knew very little about classification. So he shipped his collections from the voyage to various gentleman scientists for identification. Joseph Hooker, a highly respected botanist, undertook the heavy task of identifying the plants, and he was one of the first colleagues to whom Darwin later sent some very tentative signals about his ideas on the "transmutation" of species. Hooker responded to Darwin's hint with the comment that those most qualified to talk about what species are were those who had had "most species pass under their hands." Years later Darwin, who was laboring on the classification of a bewildering array of barnacles, wrote to Hooker with a suitably humble memory. "How painfully true is your remark that no one has hardly a right to examine the question of species who has not minutely examined many."

There are practical difficulties in identifying even the most common animals, deciding which part does what and which features recur regularly enough to assign as characteristic. These were pointed out to John James Audubon nine years after the Cuvier–Saint-Hilaire debates. He was about to depart England for the United States to begin work on a volume on North American mammals, *The Quadrupeds,* when the Reverend John Bachman wrote to him from Charleston, South Carolina: "Don't flatter yourself that this book is child's play. The birds are a mere trifle compared with this. I've been at it all my life . . . but we have much to learn in this matter. The skulls and teeth must be studied, and color is as variable as the wind—down, down in the earth they grovel, and in digging and studying we grow giddy and cross."

Hunkered over the yellow notebook on the turbino's yard and try- ing out different breathing strategies to diminish the stench, I was giddy enough without contemplating the variations among her spec- imens. But Kate was completely engaged by her dead things. She had become an expert at dealing with the dead. Through her curatorial work at the museum, she had learned how to gut, skin, and recon- struct the carcasses and skeletons of all kinds of animals, from the mice and colorful lizards of Nahuelbuta to a whale that had washed up out of the Atlantic. Even though she didn't have a Ph.D. yet, this skill had carried her into the world of formal science and brought in invitations to an international expedition to the high Andes as well as to Proyecto Zorro.

She was finicky about the state of the rodent pelts, the safekeep- ing of physical details of the teeth, and feet and tails. The numbers on the leg tag of each carcass corresponded to the numbers on one of the small vials of guts and other organs and soft tissue, which came from the same animal. I wondered at the number on the tag of one furry cylinder. "Do you know what it is?"

"This little rat? I don't know the species, but it's some kind of tree rat. I don't know many of these species. Christian probably knows a lot of them, and when I get them back to the university, Elise can help identify them."

Right now their identities were specimen numbers. Kate and I were at the beginning of the process of establishing the identity of diminu- tive research subjects and, for Elise's purposes, the identity of the ani- mals the Darwin's fox eats. When Kate's cargo arrived at the museum back in Amherst, each specimen, carcass or soft tissue, would be en- tered into the museum's catalog and laid in an array of like carcasses or intestines to await identification and permanent storage in long shallow drawers in a windowless room. Each would be tagged with its identity—species, subspecies—the place it was collected and the date. After Kate and Elise agreed on preliminary identification of the small mammals from Nahuelbuta, Kate would likely to go to the collections at Harvard to compare her examples with the bodies, skeletons, and names of the mammals from Chile in the drawers there.

The taking of specimens and the comparing of the shapes and structures is an old system for ordering the animals, and there are rooms like the ones at Amherst and Harvard in museums all over the world. Upstairs from Roland Kays's office in Albany there is a large one. He showed me around it proudly. Its drawers were filled with mice and shrews, dead songbirds. For added décor, standing on top of the cases of drawers or upright on the floor were a few larger creatures that had benefited from preservation by taxidermy—a duck, a raccoon, a black bear. "We lend these out," Roland said to make sure I understood the public service that dead animals provided. Usually, though, the researchers come to the specimens. People investigating all kinds of topics in biology, medicine, anthropology, archaeology, and even engineering come to view the bodies—I knew an anatomy professor who, in order to analyze the aerodynamics of bat flight for a Department of Defense grant, had traveled to the major museums of natural history to take the measurements of the limbs of bats in their collections.

At the time the carcasses are stowed in the drawers, their names are not always known. For some carcasses, it takes just a quick check to pin a scientific name on the specimen. For others, the process of establishing identity is drawn out, and for still others, their identities remain open.

People in Kate's line of work—the scientists who dissect, preserve, and organize specimens—are the people who sort out which tissues belongs to which part, which part does what, and which is like which. Over time, the units of comparison have become tinier and the modes of analysis more sophisticated. The duties of the job that carries the title *prosector* have spilled over to become the work of a much broader range of researchers. While zoologists are still interested in broad morphological landscapes of such visible characteristics as skull shape and size, often the microscopic territory of the molecule, particularly DNA, is the most authoritative basis on which to compare two seemingly similar animals. Intact specimens may or may not be necessary for molecular analysis, but pelts and skeletons, soft tissue, and even fossils yield evidence for classification.

One of Kate Doyle's predecessors had particular influence on how animals in the order Carnivora are classified. Early in the twentieth century, a prosector at the London Zoological Society made many first identifications of carnivores and produced anatomical comment on a great many more. Reginald Innes Pocock was in charge of dissecting and preserving for display the specimens that arrived one way or another, like the fox Darwin bonked, at the society's museum. He was on the job for a long time during a period in which scientists were harvesting a bounty of specimens. Pocock saw and described animals in every carnivore family. He published works as disparate as an ambitious catalog of the entire genus *Felis,* the cats, and a brief comment on the alisphenoid canal in civets and hyenas. From the turn of the twentieth century until well past the Second World War, what R. I. Pocock saw poured forth in publication—the maned wolf, the South African striped weasel, the feet of animals in the dog family and the bear family, the teeth of the snow leopard, the glands of the viverrids. He knew intimately the makeup of the animals and what features caused them to be allied with the other animals with which they were classified, and occasionally he had the coveted opportunity to propose a new species or even a new genus. John Eisenberg knew Pocock personally, and when I mentioned this remarkable productivity, he said, "I think he felt he owed that to the animals, to describe them." Pocock took their bodies apart. A respectful description was in order.

I saw a photograph of Pocock from the collection of the London Zoological Society. In it, Pocock, in his late fifties or early sixties, is a robust man with gray bristles covering his head and upper lip. He is wearing a three-piece suit and a homburg, and he could have been a well-satisfied broker on his way to the bank except for the fact that there was a live kinkajou clinging to his collars. It must have been a pleasure to have such close contact with something exotic yet still alive. Naming the animals and demonstrating their connections with other animals was his business, but in the case of the particular animal draped around his neck, the business was unfinished.

The kinkajou Pocock was wearing provides a wonderful demonstration of the fluidity of the classification process. Fact is established, the fact is questioned, then it's reestablished. First described in 1774 by the German biologist Johann Schreber, the kinkajou was two centuries gaining a firm foothold in any family tree. At the time the camera captured the image of Pocock and his fur stole, the kinkajou had been determined to be a kind of odd lot, the only species in the only genus in a family of canids called Cercoleptids. Before Pocock, it had been typecast as a member of the weasel family, then the civets, the mongooses, and twice—although it had the flesh-shredding premolars that identify a carnivore—as a primate. Panamanians still refer to it as *mono de noche,* night monkey. But by the time Roland began his work on the kinkajou, the animal had come to lodge pretty firmly in the Procyonids—the family that includes raccoons, the coatis of Central and South America, and the giant and red pandas, both Asian—and this classification was based in part on work done in the late 1920s by Pocock.

When the process of classification settles on the true identity of an animal—and thus defines its relationships to other kinds of animals—that satisfying moment brings biologists the security of certainty. But when a new species is discovered and validated, that is a truly exciting event. It can be a career maker, especially now when the rate of discovery of new species has slowed considerably since ships like the *Beagle* were returning home with their holds full of "natural productions" that had never been seen before. Darwin got lucky with the fox, with the frog, and with the *lauchita,* the mouse, named in his honor, and he got lucky because he was one of the earlier Old World collectors into Chile. The animal family tree has filled out, and new branches are rare. But first sightings are not impossible, and I wouldn't be surprised to find that they are a secretly cherished dream of field researchers working in wild places all over the globe.

For Kate, whose summer research had been defined as quick look-see, the specimens in the plastic boxes were a good haul. Most of the carcasses probably belonged to animals that had been seen before and had probably been named according to the highly structured rules of the International Code of Zoological Nomenclature. Although it was certainly possible that her collection of small specimens might include one dead mammal that had not been previously identified and named, the odds were against it. Still, she would go home with a nice collection of specimens. What more could a young person on the cusp of a career ask for?

A farewell gift. Elise had taken full account of Kate's seriousness of purpose, and she volunteered to go along on one of Kate's last trap-checking runs. They weren't far out on the trail when Kate's success appeared to increase dramatically. There was something alive in one of her box traps. She opened the trap and found herself looking at an unusual little mammal. It was round like a small chinchilla, which is quite common in Chile. But it lacked the long furry tail. Its pelage was a fawn color, and it had the round, warm-black eyes of a dormouse. Kate was dazzled by the rodent. A thought was forming, a wild hopeful thought. Was it possible that she had found a new animal, a new species?

Then Elise started to laugh, and this brought Kate back into her own cool head. The cuddly golden captive had been planted. It was exotic, yes. It was also a hamster.

Kate's moment of discovery and its glimpse of glory dissolved. It was the so-called golden hamster, *Mesocricetus auratus,* one of twenty-four known species of hamsters in the world. The first specimen of this animal was collected in 1839, during the same period in which Darwin collected the fox from Chiloé Island, and like the fox, this species of hamster was defined by that single specimen until the 1930s, when a few living examples were trapped in Israel and the hamster began to be bred for life in a cage. The identification of a similar animal occurring in the mountains of Chile, half a world away from the golden hamster's Eurasian origins, could have been a glittering credential for Kate Doyle. But what would it have meant for the animal?

An established scientific identify offers protection to an animal, as I discovered about Darwin's fox. Without designation as a unique species, the animal can easily slip under the sights of both the scientific and the conservation communities, and being unrecognized, can disappear with changes in the landscape where it lives. When there is no name to record in the scientific record, how are researchers to maintain an account of the animal? And what special claim does the unnamed animal have on the place it lives, the land it occupies?

Classification by species may be an artifice imposed on an unruly burgeoning of animal life, but classification limbo is not a safe place. While I was in Nahuelbuta, the animal skinned out of the pelt hanging on the clothesline had yet to be positively identified or to be confirmed as a discrete species. No one really knew where the Darwin's fit in with all foxes or, therefore, what it was. Papa, the shifty head of the parking lot family, is emphatically brindled black and gray. The chilla that Kelly and I saw, the South American gray fox, is also brindled. Parking Lot Papa has handsome russet markings on his legs and mask and ears. So does the chilla. Parking Lot Papa is smaller than the chilla, and his legs are proportionately shorter. The chilla's muzzle is broader, his ears taller in relation to his head. The chilla doesn't look all that different from the gray fox in my New York wood-lot, and at certain times of the year that North American gray fox can be easily mistaken for the red fox that lives over in the next gully. What was the Darwin's? What was this little fox that lived in Na-huelbuta and also, apparently, on Chiloé Island? Was it a species, a subspecies, or a very limited population of another fox species?

For about 150 years, the Darwin's fox had a name but no specified identity. That began to change in 1996 with an article by the entourage of American scientists who visited Chile to investigate the existence of another population of the same fox that lives on Chiloé Island. Three of the scientists now supervising Elise's work and doctoral degree—Todd Fuller, Warren Johnson, and Robert Wayne—were among the authors who referred to a "distinct, endangered species." This seemed authoritative, and certainly while I was in Nahuelbuta, the Darwin's fox's identity seemed unquestionable. The guardaparques and the people who lived on the campos around the park knew it and recognized it as its own kind of fox, and Elise and her assistants referred to it by the scientific name *Dusicyon fulvipes*. I assumed that was that: the Darwin's fox was a recognized species.

But I wanted to see how conservation biology and its committees viewed the Darwin's fox. If the Darwin's fox were "endangered," wouldn't it be on the Red List—a compilation, by the IUCN–The World Conservation Union, of plants and animals whose survival is, at least to some degree, in jeopardy? At the time, there was no men-tion of the fox in any accounting by the IUCN–The World Conser-vation Union. The group did not recognize the Darwin's fox.

It must be, I decided, that the organization, a large group with international representation and countless committees, was not fully up-to-date but would get there. I looked to the authority of the Amer-ican Society of Mammalogists. It publishes the official U.S. record of scientific findings on mammals. If there is sufficient information to report, the society authorizes the compilation of a species account. *Mammalian Species* is a serial compendium of individual descriptive summaries in strict format. It is a work that has been constantly under construction since the first account was issued in 1969. Of the estimated 4,000 species of mammals on earth, *Mammalian Species* has in its embrace 688. Accounts for twenty-five to thirty species are issued each year. New accounts are under development for species not represented; existing accounts are being updated and rehabilitated. Species accounts are revised when someone in the society makes the case that there is significant new knowledge to justify a revision. The entry for the coyote, published in 1977 and now about thirty years old, is still considered valid.

Like all the accounts, number 79, *Canis latrans,* opens with a chronological account of the various genuses to which the coyote has been assigned and moves on to a parallel history of its species classification, then to instructions for how to distinguish the coyote from other animals that look similar, the gray wolf, red wolf, domestic dog. The account summarizes key facts about the coyote's range, fossil record, its physical functions, reproduction, behavior, genetics, relationship to its habitat and to humans, before closing with a discussion of the naming and taxonomy of *Canis latrans.*

At its beginning and end, species account number 79 is concerned with names and naming. It is preoccupied with the identity of the coyote, what it is, what it does, what it has been called, what it shall be called. I tried to find the account for the Darwin's fox. There was none. There was an account for the big Chilean fox, the culpeo, but nothing for the chilla, the South American gray fox, and nothing for the Darwin's fox.

At the moment, work on *Mammalian Species* is overseen by Virginia Hayssen, a biologist at Smith College.

I asked her about the Darwin's fox.

"What's its scientific name?"

"Dusicyon fulvipes."

She looked through her list of accounts under way, trying to remember if the species had been proposed. "Nope."

I went to my Chilean field guide. "Maybe *Pseudalopex fulvipes.*"

She said, "Nope—are you sure this is a species?"

I said yes, but only because what little there was to read on the Darwin's fox always referred to the *species.* Dr. Hayssen signed off tactfully. It was good, she said, to be aware of the animal. I was now uncomfortable with what I thought I knew.

At the time, there was a species controversy heating up in the

United States that had implications for the Darwin's, with its uncertain identity. The contention focused on the so-called red wolf, and it resonated in many ways with the uncertainty surrounding the identity of the Darwin's fox. Robert Wayne, who had worked on the Darwin's and would consult with Elise on results of the DNA assays of the foxes, was a protagonist in the debate. The red wolf, *Canis rufus,* was on the verge of extinction. In 1970, there were about one hundred of these wolves left. It had become too difficult for them to hold down land, and the survivors were clinging to a confined area along the coasts of Texas and Louisiana. In 1974, the U.S. Fish and Wildlife Service began a captive-breeding and reintroduction program for the *species.* The idea was to help the red wolf reclaim its original range across the Southeast. The government rounded up as many of the straggler population as it could and sent them to a zoo in Washington state. With a good deal of public and agency celebration, the off-spring of the Washington captives were released in northeast North Carolina, in the Great Smoky Mountains, and also, as backup protection, on a few islands. They were moved to designated areas—in somewhat the same way as Native Americans were removed to reservations, the difference being, of course, that in the case of the wolves, the goal was for them to thrive.

In 1991, as the reintroductions were proceeding, Wayne published the results of a DNA study of red wolves, gray wolves, and coyotes, suggesting that the red wolf had come into the world as the result of interbreeding between gray wolves and coyotes in the eastern United States sometime after the European migration to the New World. It was a hybrid, and because animals in the canid family have shown a willingness, when under pressures that shrink their own number, to interbreed with other canid species, it was a hybrid vulnerable to repeat hybridization with coyotes, which are common across the South. This idea met with resistance from many of the supporters of the red wolf reintroduction, notably the Fish and Wildlife Service, which was spending about $1 million a year on captive breeding and reintroduction. One of the arguments mounted in defense of the red wolf as a distinct species was evidence from measurements of skulls collected before 1930 and the fossil record suggesting the *Canis rufus* was a very early species, an ancestor of both the gray wolf and the coyote.

To investigate the very-old-wolf idea, Wayne and a group of other scientists responded resourcefully. Peculiar as it sounds, the Smithsonian Institution has collected the pelts of various furbearing animals taken from 1847 on. Using pelts identified as those of red wolves trapped before 1930, the researchers compared DNA taken from red wolf hairs with the DNA of gray wolves and coyotes that lived during the same period. They found nothing to distinguish the DNA of the red wolf. This reignited the debate, and it flared into controversy. At issue were money (of course), the popular notion and scientific definition of *species,* and in the broadest sense, the use of classification to determine which animals we protect and nurture, which animals are invited onto the Ark and which are left to fend for themselves. Supporters of the red wolf were afraid of the ramifications of changing the wolf's identification as a species to that of a hybrid subspecies. It is difficult enough to get money to revive an animal on the edge of extinction and to overcome public resistance to setting predators loose in areas where they haven't been recently. If the red wolf were demoted from a species to a subspecies, what would happen to public and government support for a repopulation effort now two decades old? Would people still be willing to keep hands off and give the hybrid wolves the run of the place where they had been reintroduced?

The Endangered Species Act does not limit its benefits to species but extends protections to other kinds of animal and plant populations as well, subspecies and isolated populations. "So why," I asked Roland, "is the question of whether or not an animal is a species so important?"

"The idea of *species* is very useful," Roland said, "because the public needs something to hang on to." The scientific truth of the variations among animals and plants, he said, is that there are not clear breaks. Classification is a way of recognizing patterns of variation. "When you're at the early stages of understanding life, you need categories."

His implication was that all of us nonscientists were in these early stages. But there is truth in Roland's pragmatic take on my question: the idea of the species has become very important to the public, as least in this country and Europe. But quite frustratingly, there is no single working definition of *species* that is generally agreed upon by scientists, and especially the scientists who need to use the term most often on a day-to-day basis. The biologists I asked to explain the meaning of *species* responded with a pause followed by something like, "For the sake of argument . . ." or "Depending on what kinds of questions you're trying to get at . . ." Eventually, though, most came around to the definition proposed by Ernst Mayr as the "biological species concept": as it relates to fauna, species are "groups of actually or potentially interbreeding individuals reproductively isolated from other such groups." This reasonable proposal would seem to offer the consolations of firmness and pragmatism. But it still leaves the door open for disagreement about what constitutes a *group* and what should constitute *other such groups.*

"You have the lumpers and you have the splitters," Virginia Hayssen pointed out jovially, giving me her taxonomy of biologists. "The lumpers are the people who are willing to include a good deal of variation in a group, and the splitters—who are usually people who have spent a lot of time looking at closely related animals—attach more importance to small differences." For a lumper, a species is a fairly broad category. A splitter organizes animals into a larger number of more narrowly defined species.

The canids present another challenge to Mayr's definition in that animals recognized as species in the dog family are known to interbreed. Gray wolves mate with coyotes, and red wolves mate with coyotes, and both kinds of couplings produce fertile crossbreds. Under Mayr's definition, these hybrid animals escape classification as a species, and given that species is what the public, the IUCN–The World Conservation Union, and the Endangered Species Act seek to protect, the ambiguities in their classification could lead to ambiguities in their claim to protection on their own home ground. Perhaps the fluctuating definition of *species* is one reason that Bob Wayne and John Gittleman, writing in *Scientific American,* called for conservation efforts to be based on criteria that go beyond classification—unique functions or special traits that are not reproducible by cross-breeding.

In the case of the Darwin's fox, the evidence consisted of a few dead foxes and the blood samples Elise had drawn. The blood would likely be sent for DNA analysis to Wayne. He has devoted his career to teasing out the genetic characters of the animals he studies, and he has moved into the role occupied by Pocock and other prosectors. Where Pocock published detailed comparisons of bones in the ears of hyenas, bears, and raccoons, Wayne seeks the essential characteristics of the carnivores in strands of DNA. The advent of the polymerase–chain reaction technique, which rapidly reproduces very small amounts of DNA, made it possible for researchers like him to use physical evidence of animals—blood, hair, feces, fossils—to quantify the genetic differences between species and animals within the same species. He can detect who is related to whom and how, and by the placement of the codes, he can estimate how long these relationships have existed. His methods give him authority, by way of quantification, to say, "Yes, there is enough distinctive material here to qualify such-and-such as a species." Because of the relatively tiny differences that distinguish the DNA sequences of even one order of mammals from another order, a biologist like Wayne might be classified rather automatically as a lumper. Differences in the shape of the muzzle of two unrelated foxes and inclination to pack up or not pack up among coyotes might not be born out by significant differences in DNA. In North America, at least, this kind of analysis has the potential to upend the criteria we use to set conservation priorities and spending. But Elise thought that in Chile, the practical effects of a species designation would be more muted. When I asked her what she expected Wayne's analysis to reveal, she smiled. "I saw Bob at a conference not too long ago, and he said, kind of offhand, that he is betting the Darwin's breeds with the chilla," resulting in hybrid offspring.

What would happen if Darwin's fox DNA were determined to be not different enough from chilla DNA to allow the Darwin's fox status as a species? Elise thought about this and said, "Probably not much. Because in Chile there is no *money.* Theoretically, all foxes in Chile are protected, but without any money for conservation the species thing doesn't really matter." What was really protecting the foxes in Nahuelbuta was the park's designation as national preserve for the araucaria trees, the fact that its twenty-six square miles of cordillera were off limits.

Fortunately, as of this writing, the Darwin's has been placed on the IUCN Red List as critically endangered, and although its identity is still in flux, it seems to be approaching species status. An IUCN species account written by Elise and Jaime Jiménez declares, "the analysis of DNA of the three Chilean foxes [the Darwin's, the chilla, and the culpeo] provides strong evidence for considering the Darwin's as a legitimate species." The Red List entry, however, notes that the Darwin's "will be transferred to the genus *Lycalopex*," a small group that includes Brazil's hoary fox, which Elise and Jaime believe is the precursor of the Darwin's.

With the fox—whatever its name—now on the Red List, identification as a species will no longer have much influence on the fox's survival. But the designation science eventually settles on will affect our ideas about where the Nahuelbuta and Chiloé Island foxes fit in with other foxes and how these relationships evolved. They will determine what place the foxes hold on the carnivore family tree. Animal lineages are usually depicted with dendrograms, the same kind of laterally branching diagrams that are used to display the breeding of purebred dogs and horses. They show the regenerative process that produced a particular animal. Before it was *Pseudalopex fulvipes, Dusicyon griseus,* or *Dusicyon fulvipes,* the fox was something else. In its current manifestations in Nahuelbuta and on Chiloé, the Darwin's fox is its current arrangement of bone and tissue, on its way to being something slightly different—if it survives to evolve.

If we understand where the Darwin's fox came from, we can induce something about its evolutionary future. Here is where the uses of the long dead and the very long dead come in. By providing concrete images of the ancestors of an animal like the Darwin's fox, fossils allow us to look beyond today's carcass to infer its evolutionary lineage and something about its possible fates.

It has been said that fossils were the source of Darwin's most powerful insight, the intellectual leap that allowed him to see the linkage from geology to sex and variation. Finding fossil evidence of sea animals high in the Andes and in elevated cliffs in Scotland, he speculated on the rising and falling of great chunks of earth and seabed and began to intuit something about how these shifts acted to isolate populations of animals and plants. Later he came to locate the source of the variation and of the increasing complexity of the organisms recorded in stone as sexual reproduction. Sex was the mechanism that by its constant recombining of individuals produced over the vast scale of geological time the variety that bewildered biologists of his time, and he asserted with greater certainty that isolation—by islands, mountains, or other geological barriers—helped to fix and distill the products of this dynamic differentiation as species. As markers of this process, the long-dead have a role to play, indirect as it may be, in conservation. The classification of fossils provides the background against which contemporary families, genera, and species are categorized—or the process by which we assign the rightful places and priorities to the animals.

Because carnivores and all mammals occurred quite recently in geological time, fossil evidence of carnivore precursors is not hard to come by—witness the numerous museum displays of skeletons and skeleton imprints, teeth and claws. I was intrigued to discover that one important deposit of carnivore fossils is located not far from Bob Wayne's UCLA office in glitzy Beverly Hills under ground that now supports Saks Fifth Avenue, art museums, and a BMW dealership. While I was on Santa Cruz Island, Gary Roemer told me about the La Brea Tar Pits and urged me to see them before I went back to New York. "Very cool."

The La Brea Tar Pits have preserved in often pristine form the skeletons of Ice Age animals, including carnivores, unlucky enough to fall into the pits ten to forty thousand years ago. The tar in the pits is actually asphalt, the crudest of crude oil, that has bubbled up from the Beverly Hills reservoir, and the scene preserved in this goo is a lush landscape that housed great numbers and variety of animals. The pits have yielded up two thousand saber-tooth cats and several thousand dire wolves, which are the most common animals preserved at La Brea.

Blaire Van Valkenburgh, head of the biology department of UCLA, has extensive experience working with fossils from the pits, and she is able to make quite vivid the importance of these fossils for the carnivores living now. Working with exhumed remnants of Ice Age carnivores that lived in Beverly Hills and elsewhere, Van Valkenburgh compares their parts with parts of living animals to deduce how the ancient carnivores got around, how they killed, and what they ate. She is particularly interested in quantifying the shape and size of teeth, claws, limbs, and joints and comparing these characteristics to those of modern animals. This allows her to suggest answers to questions about how the ancient carnivores coexisted with each other—essentially the same issue that Elise, using entirely different kinds of evidence, is trying to answer about the Darwin's fox and the chilla. What Van Valkenburgh learns about the long-dead has implications for the success of the Darwin's, which is rare, imperiled, or both, in competition with the chilla.

One factor that helps validate Van Valkenburgh's investigations is the repetitiousness of evolution. The sequences that create such general features as bilateral symmetry and the multiplicity of such details as the individual claws that make up a paw recur again and again. The result is that animals with similar body forms and behaviors have emerged in different parts of the world at different times and disappeared, only to reappear somewhere else later on. Saber-tooth cats, for instance, appear fairly frequently in the fossil record, and there is a range of animals with primate-like bodies and primate food preferences that turn up in places as widely separated as Panama and Madagascar. The mechanisms that produced the very simian kinkajou, a Procyonid, repeated themselves to produce the lemur and bush babies, both primates. Of course, innovation travels with repetition and powers the changes that unfold through the generations.

In a world made perfect for Blaire Van Valkenburgh, for all carnivore biologists, in fact, fossils for all the carnivores would be laid out in contiguous slabs of stone, each ancient animal represented by the impression of its bones. For instance, ages from now the fossilized world of Nahuelbuta might look like a bas relief in which the rib cage and skull of a Darwin's is laid out near the skeleton of a lizard and one of a mouse, and not far away in the tableau, overpowering the animal scene, the thorny armor and razor leaves of the araucaria trees. Approaching the casting of the tree is the heavy outline of the puma's foot. I have left out of the tableau any traces of scrub growth because I am not sure whether this piece of the picture is weighty enough to leave an impression.

But the world was not made perfect for historical comparison. The fossil record is fragmentary. Even with new finds filling in the gaps, it is likely to remain incomplete, as Darwin noted: "we have no right to expect to find in our geological formations, an infinite number of those fine transitional forms, which on my theory have connected all the past and present species of the same group into one long and branching chain of life." One instance of absent transitional forms is that there are very few fossil specimens from the family of carnivores that includes raccoons, kinkajous, and pandas, the Procyonids. Fragmentation of the record means that we have to infer evolutionary lineages, and mistaken inferences about how to graft them together can lead to erroneous conclusions about an animal's lineage and fate.

Here is where mathematics steps in. The building and authentication of evolutionary lineages, the family trees laid out by dendrograms, has become a highly technical process, heavily dependent on mathematical simulation and statistics. Recently, John Gittleman and two colleagues published what they called a supertree that accounts for the evolution of each of the 271 living carnivores. Their dendrogram represents 60 million years. The lines in the larger, easier-to-read bifurcations are for the most part represented by the long-gone ancestors of the foxes and other carnivores, some of which are preserved at La Brea. They branch systematically with increasing frequency until, as the graph approaches the present, the divergences in it have splintered so profusely that the lines almost appear to be one thick line. One of these minute lines represents the culpeo and one the chilla—at the moment there is no line for the Darwin's. No species account by the American Society of Mammalogists. No line on the carnivore supertree.

But the dendrograms do change as new evidence is admitted. Before the latest designation of the Darwin's fox the branch on Gittleman's tree marked for the chilla would have forked off to indicate a subspecies, *Dusicyon griseus*. Now the supertree may well sprout another tiny branch after the node where foxes diverge—*Lycalopex fulvipes* or maybe *Lycalopex darwinii*.

In spite of its rather abstract theoretical project, the supertree has practical implications for the animals whose names appear on its branches: the more we know about where an animal like the Darwin's fox comes from, and the more we know about the evolutionary process though which it came to be, the more we can know about what is likely to happen to it. In terms of the conservation of an animal, what matters is not the place on the chart or the name assigned to the Darwin's but the view of the process by which it and similar animals emerged. The study of the evolution of animals is the study of what works and what does not work in a particular place, with its climate and terrain, and time. Animals with some characteristic that doesn't work—say, rigidity in diet or immediate implantation of its embryo in the female's uterus—do not *persist,* the term favored by biologists. Animals that do not persist obviously do not persist to evolve further. Their genetic heritage is sealed up, their line on the dendrogram is cut off in blankness. No further branching. This could happen to the Darwin's fox. It appears to be happening on Santa Cruz Island to the

Channel Islands fox, which when Gary Roemer began the research for his dissertation was, although more isolated, far more numerous than the Darwin's. It is the prospect of a blank spot that can get both Gary and Elise exercised.

There are several such blanks on Gittleman's supertree, dead ends that have occurred relatively recently: the Falklands wolf, the black-footed ferret, the Balinese tiger. There are a good number of others whose lines on the dendrogram are fading out. Their numbers are dwindling. The IUCN–The World Conservation Union has a series of acronyms designating the status of species that appear to be headed for trouble. The population number plus the understanding of the threats add up to the endangerment category. Beginning with LC (Least Concern), the categories head downhill through VU (Vulnerable), EN (Endangered), and CR (Critically Endangered) and reach the end with EW (Extinct in the Wild) and EX (Extinct). One of the uses John Gittleman and other evolutionary biologists make of the statistics that support their dendrograms is to project the likely rates of EX and to isolate characteristics that will predispose an animal to that most morbid of all states of death.

What are the attributes that most threaten an animal and what are the characteristics most likely to push it over the edge? For starters, there is rarity, which multiplies vulnerability to disease, predation, persecution, and habitat loss. Without beginning to account for other threats, rareness is in itself a threat. The Darwin's fox, now listed as CR, is rare. There are fewer than six hundred of them. The Ethiopian wolf, considered the most endangered of all canids, exists in an even smaller population, an estimated four hundred to five hundred.

All of this—rareness, endangerment classifications, and the models of extinction rates—is based on numbers. I asked Chris Wemmer, the biologist who heads up the Smithsonian's Conservation Research Center, where the numbers come from. He said that usually the numbers are based on survey questionnaires sent to researchers who specialize in a particular animal. The surveys ask: How many do you think there are? And how is that different from five years ago? Actual censuses are infeasible, and the system is wide open to subjectivity. In the case of the Darwin's fox, surveys might be sent to Elise and Jaime Jiménez, and a population number would be extrapolated from their two estimates. The method seems not much more sophisticated than

Darwin's journal entry on the population of the fox he bopped: "a fox of a kind said to be peculiar to the island and very rare in it." But the scientific community has had to content itself with best-estimate figures, and Wemmer, in fact, presides over a campus that houses and breeds many animals counted this way and considered rare and endangered.

As I think of Darwin's report of his fox's uncommonness, I realize how closely place is linked with population. Animals move into place, stay and adapt if they can, head out again if they can't. Although Elise suspects there may be Darwin's foxes in other parts of Chile, the two places known to support the fox—a rainy island and a mountainous land preserve that is essentially a landlocked island—have something in common, dense undergrowth. This is what works for the fox or what meshes with some capacity of the fox. In Nahuelbuta this undergrowth protects the diminutive carnivore from the eyes of the puma and the culpeo, but on Chiloé, death by predation isn't much of a problem for the fox. There is something about a heavy shrubby understory that allows the animal a tolerable standard of living. At the moment, fortunately, the Darwin's does not appear to be challenged by starvation, disease, or to any unbalancing extent, larger carnivores. What limits its numbers might be nothing more than the fact that it likes a certain amount of cover and a certain size area of the stuff.

But areas of shrubby understory are being chipped away, and the Red List names habit loss via logging as the most important threat to the fox. The patch of forest in the cordillera is protected but only up to its edges—what do foxes know about legal boundaries?—and Chiloé is subject to the pressures of resort development. Both are made more frail by the fact that they are insular.

7 ≶ Here's Where I Get Off

ONE NIGHT IN NORTHERN PANAMA NEAR A PLACE ON THE Caribbean Ocean called Fort Sherman, I found myself dangling two hundred feet over the rain forest floor in a steel cage and scared pretty much witless. The cage was about four feet square, and there were three other people with me, including Roland, who was enjoying himself. The only way for me to deal with hanging so high in the air, nothing solid underfoot, was to look up. Fortunately, it was not really possible to judge how far down the ground was. It was dark, and the lines of perspective were nearly invisible. Roland kept popping from one side of the cage to the other, making it rock gently and creak on the hook that held it over the trees. I could have killed him.

The cage was the business end of a huge construction crane set in the rain forest near the Caribbean. It was cast out over the trees by a cable let down from the immense steel arm of the crane. In the hands of Edwin, who had driven our truck on the two-hour drive from Gamboa, the cage on its cable traveled out to the end of the arm. The basket ran up and down. The crane arm swung in a semicircle. Occasionally the hook creaked or the machine groaned. The cage's travels were dictated via walkie-talkie from the corner nearest mine by Vibeke, who managed the crane for the Smithsonian Tropical Research Institute (STRI). In the corner across from me was Stephanie, a young botanist who had been up in the crane's basket many times but never at night, because this was the first time anyone could remember the crane sweeping the treetops at night.

After a year talking about it, we had come down to Panama so that I could see the kinkajous Roland had studied and write a magazine article about them. It was my last trip for wildlife research, and fortunately, it was that rare trip where everything goes right. In the biological abundance of the Canal Zone, it was easy to see the synchronization among all the features of natural history on which Roland, Elise, and Gary sought data—territory, food, breeding and family, species— and how smoothly these are divvied up. This was mostly due to Roland's planning. Our time in the Zone was limited, and he optimized the opportunities for scientific play. We had been in the country for about ten days, trapping and tracking in Parque Nacional Soberanía, Roland shinnying up three-story trees and me watching. Roland had carefully orchestrated our days so that I saw not only the kinks but more animals of more kinds than I realized existed. I had to keep lists, and my notebooks filled up with the names of birds and rodents and mammals like the agouti, which looks like a long-legged guinea pig with cloven feet, and the coati, the snout-down, tail-up relative of the raccoon that forages in little herds that seem to be steered in unison by their long, erect, striped rudders. I knew I would probably never see these animals again, never have the opportunity to see them living together, and—ignoring the fact that the Zone was filled with scientists who had already documented the animals with authority—I tried to get it all down as precisely as possible. A couple of days of scribbling and I had firsthand experience of the motive behind taxonomy. Although classification has many theoretical and political justifications, it is essentially a practical endeavor. You need some way to sort out what you are seeing. For his part, Roland had been grabbing up natural artifacts, seeking information in every encounter on every foray, and I began to see more of the intellectual machinery and the aspirations that keep him in motion. It had been a wonderful time, until the ride in the basket of the canopy crane.

When the gondola was cranked up as high as it could go, snug to the steel arm, it was possible to see the length of the Zone, the strip of land and the canal that bisects Panama on the shortest path between the Atlantic and Pacific. Straight out ahead of me were the lights of the ravaged slums of tax-free Colón, and straight behind me Panama City glowed, miles away on the Pacific. The purpose of the canopy crane and the one like it at the other end of the canal in Panama City is rain forest research. Guarding patches of forest at either end of the canal, Panama's largest commercial enterprise, the canopy cranes are emblematic of the country's commitment to preserving yet making the most of the natural abundance that surrounds its cities, where poverty and entrepreneurial success, profusion of peoples and cultures, and a search for national identity mingle in confusion.

Panamanians are in a flush of pride over their jungles, their amazing birds, their whimsical mammals, their butterflies and their frogs decked out like Mardi Gras. Biodiversity and its preservation are a national preoccupation, along with awareness of the commercial possibilities in the rain forest enterprise, and science is practically an industry. Scientists from all over the world have been congregating there for nearly a century, and there is a utopian intensity about conservation.

Because conservation is a national priority, the Panamanians are trying to do the land thing right. While Panama's cities seemed crowded and pocked with urban decay, rot that trailed in with the country's long succession of occupiers and colonizers, there is a peculiar abundance of land. This is also an aftereffect of colonization.

In the Zone itself, which was relinquished by the United States only recently, the Panamanians are still figuring out what to do with the land and buildings left open to them. Outside the Zone, in western Panama, the rain forest north of the rugged cordillera that runs from the Zone to Costa Rica is undeveloped; the eastern third of the country is wilderness, sparsely populated and essentially ungoverned. In the United States I am always aware of land being consumed by human activity. In the lake country where I live, in the Pine Bush Preserve, and even on Santa Cruz Island, which a fence now severs, there is always some human purpose asserting domain over wild places. While it is possible that even in Panama nature is losing ground, I didn't sense this. Certainly the animals aren't being pushed out.

We were staying in Gamboa, the little town that serves as the port for the ferry that runs three times a day to Barro Colorado, the island preserve maintained by the Smithsonian Tropical Research Institute. Based in Panama City on Ancon Hill, STRI has been a powerful influence in Panama for the past ninety years, and Gamboa is its suburban outpost. Many of the people who live there are scientists and graduate students. The rest of the people are of a fairly broad run of Zonians, that mix of Panamanians (who are themselves an cosmopolitan mix of native Central Americans with European, Asian, and Caribbean peoples), expatriates from all over the world (whichever people happened to have passed through the canal), and their descendents.

The town was laid out in spirals and cul-de-sacs on a hill beside

the canal that Roland allowed was created by the build-up of dredg-
ings from the canal. In spite of the fact that the Zone has been returned to Panama by the United States, many of the houses in Gamboa are still owned by the Smithsonian. All look very similar, a kind
of standard-issue beach house, raised on piers, painted gray, and
topped off with deeply sloped hip roofs. At the top of the hill, the center of town, was a bigger place, three stories, that housed some STRI
offices, graduate student apartments, and equipment and the com-
puters for the whole community. The backyards were buffered by thin
strands of rain forest, and the densely matted lawns were traversed by
the prodigious trails tramped out by the leaf-cutter ants that were
everywhere. At the foot of the hill, not far from the ferry landing, a
set of gleaming new glass structures looked like tall greenhouses.
These were growth chambers used by the scientists who work on the
area's rampant plant life.

The scientific culture was as lush as the vegetation, and its diversity as intense as that of the fauna. Every morning about seven the doors
of the houses opened, and scientists and graduate students descended
to street level and walked down the hill to the waiting ferry in a line
as predictable as the lines made by the leaf-cutters. Every Thursday
there was a "Bambi," an informal presentation in the research center
on Barro Colorado. Every Tuesday there was a more formal presentation by a scientist at the STRI headquarters in Panama City. Every
Friday the scientists played Frisbee in Gamboa. Weekends and some
weeknights they gathered to eat and drink. I was amused to think that
this intense interaction of scientists would have set Darwin's socially
timid guts roiling.

People in town speculated frequently about which of the two seasons we had arrived in. It was late November, and the wet season,
when rain is relentless, was winding down. But the dry season was not
yet controlling. It rained every day, on and off, but not very hard. The
humidity was enervating. My arms and legs felt weighted, and with
any exertion I seemed to gasp for air like a landed fish. Roland seemed
unhampered by the dense air or by anything else.

From the outset, things went easily. What had been difficult in
Chile and New York came readily. What was scarce or sparse in those
places was numerous and burgeoning in Panama. We found kinkajous right away, and other animals presented themselves obediently as

if they were taking cues from somebody offstage. No doubt this was due in part to the fact that Roland was returning to familiar animals in familiar places. But also it was because of the abundance. The place was crowded with species and with the many members of each. It was a kind of theme-park Eden.

The first night we went out with spotlights and headlamps to the Pipeline Road. The road, which is referred to in most of the tourist publications as "the famous Pipeline Road," was a maintenance route for an oil pipeline built by the United States during the Cold War to transport fuel from one coast to the other in case of an attack on the canal. The pipeline and the road run parallel to the canal from Colón on the Caribbean to Panama City on the Pacific. The pipe has never been used, and the road is now no more than twin ruts and passable only in the sections where the plank bridges haven't rotten out. If the road is famous, it is famous among birders for the abundance of brightly colored birds that swoop across the road from treetops on either side.

At night most of the birds are asleep, and the only colors in the forest were from the eyes of animals picked up by our spotlights. Roland drove the little four-wheel-drive truck, and I stood up behind the cab with a hand-held spotlight. "Look for a balsa," he instructed. In the daylight Roland had showed me a tall balsa tree in Gamboa. It had heart-shaped leaves and was just beginning to put up big white flowers. The kinks love the nectar. He threw the truck into gear, and it lurched off fast enough to cut a breeze in the dense air that sank over the road. The palms and hardwoods and the shrubs with swords for fronds streamed past on either side.

A few hundred yards past the gate, Roland realized that the balsas along Pipeline Road hadn't advanced to flower. No problem. He stopped the truck, turned off the lights, and got out to listen, sitting on the tailgate in the dark. "If there's one any place near, we'll hear it," he said, and I assumed he meant the kinks would make themselves heard with calls, cries, something vocal. After a few minutes, he turned on his headlamp and set out in the road ahead of the truck, the light disappearing with him. But it wasn't long before a speck of it reappeared and grew with his approach.

"There's a fruiting fig," he announced, and we drove on a half mile to stop in front of the fig tree's enormous trunk. Way up, thirty feet or more, the tree began branching, and it grew more complex and more voluminous until it almost obscured our view of the night sky. Scattered widely on the road were a few green figs about the size of hickory nuts. We put on our headlamps and switched on the beams.

"Hear that?" he said. I didn't. I could hear only a rattling of leaves a ways off, and the business with the headlamps was amusing me. Turning them up, snuffing them out. I told Roland it reminded me of the ghost in Dickens's *Christmas Carol* with his extinguisher cap.

"Hear that?" he insisted.

Only a faint clattering in the canopy.

"You mean the leaves?"

"That's his shit coming down." Roland trained his beam on the area of leaves where the sound seemed to be coming from. The light momentarily ignited two orange orbs. "See him?"

I did, and the kinkajou saw us. He stopped traveling the branch and peered down at us, the Day-Glo eyes regarding us mildly. He was larger than a squirrel, tawny with a long, muscular tail and a flat, foreshortened face that instantly brought to mind a TeleTubby. But he was far more appealing than a cartoon character made to mesmerize toddlers. In my unscientific opinion, he was downright adorable. But a kinkajou, nonetheless. I could see why the kinkajou had confounded taxonomists for almost three centuries. Part squirrel, part monkey, he worked the balsa tree with the affectionate avidity of a human baby.

The kink was not much concerned about the strong light or the strange animals below, and he went on working his way sinuously along the branch, among its leaves, looking for something to eat. I was transported. Here finally was an animal that made itself available to be seen. A clatter of leaves over on the other side of the tree announced the presence of a second kinkajou. Roland went directly to the feces and brought the stuff back for me to see. It looked like the figs on the road, as if they had been run though a food processor for a second and sauced with a translucent jelly. Its low-cal diet and the kinkajou's hasty digestive mechanism mean that once his hard day's night begins, the kink has to travel constantly and spend a lot of energy seeking food.

The two kinkajous' travel was amusing. They were fast, slick climbers that could ascend in an instant to the highest, most fragile branches, then hang by their tails, drop and swing to change direction.

Before Roland went down to Panama to begin research on the

kinkajou, the scientific literature presumed that the kinkajou—like so many other shoot-'em-one-at-a-time animals—was solitary. He didn't set out to investigate this assumption or to focus necessarily on kinkajou social life. But his success with traps hoisted into big trees and a willingness to travel the rain forest at night gave him the means to observe the kinks—he could shoot more than one at a time. Once he had collared enough kinkajous, he tracked the radio signals until he found his subjects. Often when he trained the beam of his headlamp high into the canopy, he found the kinks in small, close groups, grooming and squabbling and having sex a hundred feet up. Life high in the leafy byways was decidedly not solitary. It was a floating party.

While it was true, he found, that the kinkajou does spend a good deal of its time alone, that is because of the distance a kink has to travel to find and consume enough food. But there are many nights when several of the foraging kinkajous arrive in the same treetop and let their quests for fruit and nectar gradually draw them together into close body contact.

These are kinkajou families. They spin out from the female, who, like the female hyena, is the linchpin of her family and its social life. She lives in the company of two unrelated males and the pups she bears, and she has the distinction among all female carnivores of establishing the family's territory. She copulates more frequently, or at least effectively, with one of the males, the dominant, and over the years, the paternity of her pups, which she usually delivers at the rate of one a year, reflects this preference.

She is promiscuous, *promiscuity* being a term like *persecution* that biologists use without its usual moral load. Promiscuity is what animals do, and it provides an efficient means of distributing genes and, along with them, diversity. Among carnivores a chaste mother-father-pup configuration has been something of a paradigm, partly because that's what we were able to observe and partly because that's what our rigid notions about what a family should look like caused us to expect to observe. But for an increasing number of animals in this family, evidence of adultery—so-called "extra-pair mating"—has come to light. Most of the first cases observed involved male animals. But if promiscuous males are a dime a dozen, so too, accumulating evidence reveals, are females. The female kinkajou is promiscuous within her family group. Each of the males, however, focuses loyally on that female. If

her pup is a female, the pup will leave the family and its home territory when she matures, and she will set out along the leafy byways that
link the canopy and stake out an area of trees as her own. A male pup
matures and moves into the territory and social interchange with the
group of a nearby female unrelated to his mother. It is a *matriarchy,*
but this word, like *promiscuous,* is devoid of the implications we usually give it.

What is unusual about the female kinkajou is that, as soon as she
is sexually mature, she leaves her family group to search out new territory. Among carnivores and other mammals, these territorial functions are almost exclusively male prerogatives. We sat on campstools
watching the kinks nose hungrily about the foliage of the fig tree.

"So then what animal eats the kinkajous?" I wondered. Pretty
much nothing, it turns out. Roland reminded me that they have no
serious predators. They are not on the hit lists of hawks and eagles because they forage at night, and although they may occasionally end
up in the stomach of a hungry jaguar or jaguarundi, they usually climb
too fast and too high into branches too delicate to bear the weight of
a larger predator.

If there was only *eat* and no *be eaten* for the kinks, why didn't they
just eat and reproduce until they took over the fig tree, then the neighboring trees, and eventually the Parque Nacional Soberanía? The answer to my question about what keeps the kinks in balance with their
neighbors was *energy.* Kinkajous are a convenient demonstration of
the energy economics of the Resource Dispersion Hypothesis. In the
kinkajou matriarchy, the female's role involves more burden than
power. All the time she works to stake out and hold her territory, to
bear her young and nurse the pup, she survives on low-energy food.
She needs more energy than the male needs, and she has to travel farther to satisfy these needs. She can't sustain many pups, and this is the
reason she usually gives birth to only one. She has to work harder than
the male, scrambling along the high, leafy byways all night to get
enough food for herself and her pup.

No guarantees, but for the most part, not much danger. The narrow niche occupied by the kinkajou is a cul-de-sac in the rain forest
food web. Predator manqué.

"I think where they fit in," Roland said about the local forest, "is
through seed dispersal. They eat all this fruit, then they run around

in the trees. The shit rains down and—you saw the stuff—leaves un-
damaged seeds on the forest floor."

Watching the avid grazing of the kinks, I became aware that there
were other eyes and reflective patches. Other animals were visible in
the fig tree. As I trained a beam on each one to point it out, I found
Roland already knew it was there: *"Didelphis virginiana*—the same
possum you have in New York only smaller . . . *Caluromys derbianus,*
another possum." A mouse for which he couldn't pull out the Latin
name. A spider. These were the animals of the night shift acting out
how sympatry, the sharing of territory, takes place over time. It was
their time to shine and to eat. Every creature in the huge, leafy dome
was looking for food, and Roland himself went to the truck and
started digging around in his pack. "I could use something to eat."

The next morning iridescent hummingbirds and brilliant blue
honeycreepers mobbed the syrup feeder hanging from the clothesline
in the yard, and Roland was down in the kitchen of the borrowed
house boiling up more water and sugar. The day before he had bought
a huge stalk of bananas to bait the kinkajou traps, and he had set out
one of the riper ones on a tray feeder that swung from the line. A
stolid green motmot eyed it from a tree branching over the yard, and
four Geoffroy's tamarins (for Geoffroy Saint-Hilaire) advanced on it
cautiously from the lowest branches of another tree. With their wiz-
ened black heads and fringed faces, they looked like aging curates.
One of the little monkeys tested the clothesline, creeping out a little
ways from the screw eye that anchored the line, and the motmot,
unable to tolerate the competition for the banana, flew down under
the cloud of blue and green birds swarming the syrup feeder to the
hanging tray and the prize. The monkeys considered the motmot's
success, and as soon as the bird flew up from the tray, two of them
scrambled out the line to hang by their feet and grab at the feeder.
The tray rocked, and a piece of banana fell down to the grass. An
agouti, which is sometimes kept as a dooryard pet in Gamboa, was
hovering in the bushes at the edge of the yard. It ambled out on the
lawn and snatched the banana tidbit. Every animal on cue to demon-
strate the efficiency of this lively hothouse.

We stowed plastic bags of bananas and the wire cage traps we had
brought over on the ferry from Barro Colorado Island in the bed of
the pickup, and we started for Roland's research site way out on

Pipeline Road in a place called Limbo. In the daylight Pipeline Road's two overgrown tracks gave off clouds of vapor. Enormous blue mono butterflies lingered over the road, and a toucan crossed in front of us. Roland pointed out a puffbird and the calls of antbirds, antpittas, and antwrens.

We left the truck at a stream where the bridge had rotted through, carried our gear and the cages to another truck STRI left parked on the other side, and drove over a couple more streams until we came to another dark, slippery bridge with a hole in it. From there we proceeded on foot. After we crossed the wide, shallow stream of the Limbo River, we began to see flags of fluorescent pink surveyor's tape tied in the trees by an earlier group of ornithologists. They had measured an area of about one square kilometer and in it created a grid of trails at regular intervals. This was Limbo Plot, where Roland had spent hundreds of nights. Although it was named for the Limbo (meaning edge, I think, in this context) River, I found the name delightfully apt in the Dantean sense. Dim, dense, humid—and once inside, I had no idea where I had gotten or how to find my way out.

"Don't get too far ahead of me," I said. "I'll never find my way back to the road."

Roland thought I was trying to be funny. But to me, the "trails," as he called them, were indistinguishable openings in the foliage. They were immediately evident to him. He knew every sizable tree in the plot, and he whacked away happily with his machete at the understory plants that had grown up enthusiastically to choke the trails. He noticed things far more often than I did. It may have been partly because he knew this piece of rain forest and what it might offer. But still, he was good at seeing things and getting hold of them, pulling down specimens faster than Darwin with his bird gun. He would make a little dive with his hand cupped. Then he would turn his hand over to show a black-and-green frog struggling there, or a yellow snake, or the husk of a big insect amazingly intact. I have a photo of redheaded Roland with the ring in his ear and a small snake lifted up in front his face and his big grin. He showed me a termite nest as large as a piñata and, looking into it from the opening at the bottom, told me this was the way a new species of bat had been discovered recently. The researcher had come down to Panama to fill in for another scientist for just a few weeks, and during that time she had noticed a bat that seemed to go in and out of a termite nest. When she looked, she discovered that the bat was roosting there among the termites. "She was so lucky," Roland said.

We were very lucky, too. We left six cage traps hoisted high in trees Roland selected for their open architecture. For some, he had been able to create the hoist line by using a slingshot to fire parachute cord over a likely branch. For others he had had to climb up into the tree and drop the hoist line over the branch. His T-shirt would be soaked in sweat before he reached the first fork. The next morning we found a kinkajou in one of the traps. We let the trap down, and Roland sedated the kink. It was a female, and she lay stretched out in my lap while Roland measured and weighed her, took blood, and fit the radio collar. I had a very close, satisfying look at her. Golden fur with a hint of frizziness and a darker stripe down the back and tail, which was surprisingly muscular. Her claws were very long and curved, her ears quite short, and as promised ahead of time, there was a vertical groove in each of her upper carnassial teeth. When she regained consciousness, she came to all at once and streaked out of the open cage for the top of the nearest tree. We named her Lupe and used the radio receiver to track her nightly movements in the upper reaches of Limbo.

The ease with which things were happening in Parque Soberanía made comparison with Nahuelbuta unavoidable. The place where Elise worked was unforgiving, and the rewards for the research thin. She was seeking a rare animal in a forest where nature had been tight-fisted, and she was still operating with a learner's permit. Where Roland worked in Panama, everything, including the animals, was more plentiful. But while he was getting his license, he too had to work through failure and frustration and spend hundreds of overnights walking around the rain forest with his head tipped back, looking up into the dark—"and now I have really strong neck muscles." On one of these nights, the kinkajou Roland was tracking paused for a while in one tree. He sat down to wait, and his headlamp shone down on a green snake curled cozily between the footprints he had just left. A deadly fer de lance. Neither his nor Elise's lot was an easy berth, and I think the crucial difference between their experiences had to do with support for the scientific enterprise. Elise worked in a rural area, remote from other scientists or even people with education, and she spent a good deal of time smoothing the way for her research with any government agency with any hold on Nahuelbuta or the Darwin's fox, giving talks to guardaparques from other parks in Chile, making cappuccino. In Panama, science has been an influential sector since even before the Panamanians realized that the way to reap the most from the rain forest and the cloud forest was to conserve them. Having helped establish conservation, science is expected to further it. Science is, in fact, just plain expected. The Chinese woman who runs the produce stand hardly noticed when I went in to buy a stalk of bananas four feet long. She just nodded pleasantly: "Ah, Rolando." Resources appropriated to science are justified by its product, fact, and Roland is accustomed to taking what is at hand and putting it into the service of fact. If he can get hold of a solar cell and a video-cam, he makes a video trap. If he spots a black-and-green appaloosa frog, he grabs it.

When the time we had allowed for trapping and tracking had almost run out, Martin Wikelski, a biologist from Princeton, and his friend Franz Kümmeth, an engineering student from Germany, arrived. They had come to help Roland set up an experimental telemetry system on Barro Colorado Island that would be capable of tracking and recording simultaneously the movements of many animals of different species. The scheme used radio receivers on multiple towers to pick up the signals of radios on collars, glued to the backs of birds, maybe even implanted in snakes. The signals would be collected and downloaded by software used for tracking bus fleets, and the movements of all the creatures would be revealed to someone sitting in front of a computer monitor. Martin, a dark-haired and thin German, had wide interests that encompassed physiology, behavior, and a number of species. His running shoes were beat, and his sense of humor ready at the surface. I liked how respectful he was toward Franz, who was much younger with no degrees yet and who would be responsible for the actual construction of the radio system.

The idea for the towers wasn't new. Bill Cochran had built a tracking system using towers in Illinois in the 1960s and met Martin later when the two worked together in Illinois in the late 1990s. Now he was building the receivers for the towers on Barro Colorado. The software had been around for a little while and just happened to be produced by a company owned by the father of a friend of Roland's. The ideas were there—spawned by the frustration of tracking individual animals on foot—the technology was close, and all it took to string together the components was the enthusiasm of Martin and Roland.

"He's still young," Bill Cochran said in appreciation of Roland, and then, having himself devised a radio antenna by tying a fifteen-foot gold wire to an albatross, he said without a trace of irony, "Doesn't know when a thing can't be done."

I tried to bury my suspicions. To me the project sounded about as appealing as cell towers, too closely related to land development—build, build, build. "That's a lot of scaffolding," I said to Roland, "a lot of metal."

He wasn't concerned about imposing the complicated artifice on Barro Colorado Island.

"Will they let you build all that stuff on the island?" If a leaf falls on Barro Colorado, there is a scientist with a personal stake in the event and a community with a passionate commitment to keep the leaf where it falls.

"I suppose." Roland was still working on formal permission for the project. "As long as we don't cut down any trees."

Martin and Franz had time to kill before ferrying over to Barro Colorado with Roland, and they volunteered to help dismantle our trap line and haul the equipment back to the truck. It was the hottest, dampest day yet, and Franz and I were still registering the shock of the humidity. Even walking seemed to require a good deal of effort. But at the base of a steep hill Martin looked up, dropped the trap he was carrying, and sprinted. It was amazing to see anyone run in the deadeningly wet air. But then Roland took off close behind.

"What is it?" Franz and I were fifty yards back. We scanned the crest of the hill. Martin seemed to be chasing something. A tail appeared briefly, then Roland ran in from the other side. By the time Franz and I reached the crest of the hill, Roland was aiming the video camera into the fork of a tree near the road, where the anteater had retreated. It showed us its back and turned its face only once to glare resentfully down its pale needle nose.

"Just a little too far away," Martin explained. "Usually all you have to do is grab the tail and lift it up."

The next day I relayed Martin's wisdom to a local nature guide. "If you do that," he promised solemnly, "if you lift them up by the tail, they will *pee* on you." But a little pee wouldn't have deterred Martin or Roland. The anteater certainly wasn't the first they'd seen, but it was *another* anteater to be seized and looked at.

Roland's understanding of truth about the anteater, and Martin's, is the compilation of facts about the animal. For Roland, fact is a goal in itself. If I asked a question he couldn't answer immediately, he began at once to strategize about how to gain the answer. "You know, you could do a really neat study of that by . . ."

Scientific facts are established by a call-and-response process. A new fact is arrived at, say, during dissertation research like Roland's and Elise's, and published. Then it is questioned and tested, and as this happens, it gradually gains authority as well as nuance and is passed on. Cuvier to Darwin. Darwin to Pocock. Pocock to Eisenberg. Eisenberg to Gittleman, and so it goes, Gittleman to Kays. Eventually, as Francis Bacon promised, the accumulation of fact, catalyzed by a sprinkling of hypothesis, amounts to a state of knowledge, and that kind of knowledge was what Roland was going for.

We were sitting in traffic just outside Gamboa, waiting for our turn to cross a single-lane bridge and talking about another wildlife biologist, an ornithologist. Roland found him remarkable for the range of his knowledge. He admired him as something of a phenomenon. "He knows just about every bird in the world, and he's seen most of them—maybe all of them by now. That's what I'd like to do only with mammals. I'd like to know every mammal in the world." His keenness is something quite fresh, and his assumption that all is not known but can be is quite innocent even if a little rapacious.

Sometimes I have trouble keeping up with Roland. He thinks very fast and pondering can make him impatient. For him, the most scathing pejorative is *boring*. His graduate seminar on the writings of Darwin had been *boring*. Ditto for le Carré's *Tailor of Panama*— which I found so suspenseful when I was listening to it in the car that I missed my exit and had to drive sixty miles out of my way.

Of course, in order to prowl around Panama snatching up snakes and insect hulls and anteaters, in order to get his license, he has had to endure a lot of *boring* stuff: the earlier catalogers of animals, the early speculators on the sources of natural variety, the first gringo scientists drawn into Panama by Central America's plenty. Fact has always been the packaging for scientific ideas, and while many of the ideas witnessed by the facts are very exciting, their literary vehicles have for centuries been freighted with heavy, overloaded nouns. Roland is by training a survivor of this literature, but now that his work is a product of it he can afford to be far more interested in fresh fact, wriggling up close at hand, than in the eminences of biology, their texts setting out obsolete theories, their visions.

To me, it seems entirely possible that if he holds up physically, Roland Kays *will* know every mammal in the world. He is willing to put any resource into the service of factual discovery, so I was not surprised when he came up with the idea of hunting kinkajous with the canopy crane. Maybe I should have at least paused to consider the proposal. But I didn't. I had witnessed his solar cell hitched to the digital video in the Pine Bush Preserve and, in the Adirondack Park, his recruitment of a fingerprinting expert recently retired from the New York State Troopers. These imaginative schemes had worked out, and coming from Roland, hunting kinkajous by night in the canopy crane seemed entirely feasible. Like coyotes in the freezer locker or schnapps in the kinkajou traps, it was an uninhibited idea that would probably work. Roland had reserved the crane weeks in advance. He thought it might prove easier or more telling to see the kinks at or above their own height in the huge trees where they foraged, and he wanted to scout good vantages for the photographer who would arrive months later.

I had been dreading the crane since before light that morning. Before I left the States I made it clear to Roland that I was afraid of high places, and I could have stayed behind at the borrowed house near the canal. He would have been polite—or at least he wouldn't have shamed me. But it's not unusual for me to ask to try something without considering how I will respond to what happens. I wanted to go along to see whatever Roland was going to see. I couldn't stand the thought that the night would bring an exciting encounter that I would miss—and he wouldn't.

To get to the crane, five of us sat shoulder to shoulder in a Smithsonian truck for two hours, while Edwin dodged the enormous potholes on the highway that skirts the canal and Lake Gatun, veering out of the way of the oncoming cars and trucks that were dodging the potholes on their side of the road. After we crossed the Gatun Locks, we turned north toward the Caribbean into the forest preserve that surrounds Fort Sherman at the broad northern mouth of the canal.

Here the road ceased, and the track Edwin negotiated with the truck was as *horrible* as any of the roads in Nahuelbuta. In certain passages it would have been faster to walk over the boulders. It was near-dark by the time we reached the stone cottage where the guards lived in rotating shifts.

Before we walked down the steep slippery creek bed to the hollow where the crane stood, I noticed Edwin changing out of the open-collar shirt he had worn out from Panama City and putting on a tank top. I was extremely nervous, and in the maneuvers that took us up on the concrete pad where the gondola rested I lost track of everyone, including Edwin, but me. Vibeke checked out radio contact, and the crane began to lift the gondola cage. Aside from an occasional ominous creak or groan, the ride up through the canopy was silent.

"How are you doing?" Roland asked.

"I'm terrified."

"You can sit down."

I tried that. I still had a detailed view of the branches we were approaching, but I felt idiotic and pulled myself upright again to stand in a corner clutching the steel railing. We glided close to the highest forks of several trees, where Roland was trying to pick up eye shine with the spotlight. Then back out of that particular convolution in the canopy and down to a younger tree. Up and over, across the entire treescape.

"Who are you talking to?" I asked Vibeke. "Who is running this thing?"

"Edwin," as if that was perfectly evident, and she pointed down the long arm of the crane to a steel-and-glass compartment fixed at the intersection of the arm and the tower. My knees tried to buckle. The man in the booth was so high up. I looked up to avoid any further sensation of the altitude. Everyone else was looking *out*. The spotlight probed the billowing branches and foliage. It was like being under the sea at night.

Roland began to ask for Edwin to make more complicated maneuvers with the gondola. We had glimpsed only the surface of the dark reef, and he wanted to use the machine's full capacity to explore. If there were any of Panama's many birds and arboreal animals within the sweep of the crane, they were making themselves invisible.

"I'm surprised we're not seeing more," Roland said.

I had seen enough. I closed my eyes as our craft glided over the canopy. But it did seem odd. We had spotted a good number of kinks from the ground. You would think that moving up to the height where they lived would help us find many more.

Roland saw another channel in the foliage that he thought was a likely hangout for kinkajous. He was going for it. The rest of us were going with him. The gondola drifted on the sea of dark. It slowly dipped and rose, making what seemed endless investigations of the coves and fjords in the foliage. Like everything else in Panama—the hothouse rain forest, the abundant animal life, the scientific culture— the crane gondola's night passage was intense. I knew that the slow, agonizing flight would be over in a matter of the hours and minutes it took for the spotlight batteries to run down. And I knew that my trip to Panama was coming to an end, and when it did, I wouldn't re- member the fear, just the fantastical view of the top of the rain forest.

Roland scanned with our big spot, seeking out likely holes in the canopy, dark places where the architecture of the trees opened. He wasn't finding any animals. I hoped he would get tired of this and ask Vibeke to ask Edwin to lower us down to the concrete pad beside the tower. But his enthusiasm and my terror continued.

At some point before the spotlights flickered out, the state of be- ing suspended in fear in a metal basket forced a few moments of ob- jectivity on me. I considered Roland and Elise friends, and the ques- tions and data they pursued were by now as familiar to me as home. I tried hard to get this all down right, because their work and their facts were important to the survival of the animals they studied. Yet, when it came to the poking and prodding of nature that every inves- tigation of natural history since the term was invented has necessi- tated—researchers have to tickle the thing so it will roll over and they can see what it is—I hesitated, because in some lingering sense I was still troubled about manipulating living things to flush out fact. I felt guilty about my misgivings because Roland had put out a lot to bring me to this abundant place and show me its wealth of animals. Maybe I was out of place, not fit to be dangling in the canopy crane to gather fact because like Rat and Mole coming upon Pan in *The Wind in the Willows,* I still had too much awe in me. I was still an amateur and didn't have enough of the ruthlessness of science.

But somebody has to be ruthless because conservation depends on scientific fact. In Panama there were enough facts of nature to keep Roland and the other people who mined them for a living digging for a few more centuries. What the facts usually yield are outlines of a life, and these most often coalesce into a silhouette, not a portrait, of the animal. There have been studies, especially of primates, that provide much deeper knowledge of an animal's life. But these are not the usual, and it is not necessary that research achieve this as the usual. It is the silhouettes and their arrangement as an ecological diorama that are essential.

I had been after something more when I tried to follow the coyote on horseback, when I stepped off the packet boat to Santa Cruz Island, flew down to Chile and now to the coast of Panama. I was after more intimate knowledge of the coyote and the fox and ways to get that kind of knowledge for other wild animals. I wanted to get the particulars of what it is to be a fox or a coyote or a kinkajou, to appreciate the differences between fox-ness, coyote-ness, kinkajou-ness, and human-ness. I wanted something like what David Macdonald had in mind when he started off with a red fox on a leash: "I wanted to get under the animal's skin." But as I considered all this from the scary vantage of the cage on the long steel boom, I could see that, while this kind of knowledge would be kind of exquisite, it is not possible. To make this kind of understanding a goal would undermine conservation. Field studies take years as it is, and while they're under way, the places that support wild animals are increasingly claimed by humans. A goal like mine is an unnecessary distraction. I had to accept this and expect something more like what David Macdonald came around to and now requires of his graduate students: "something useful." What is useful is to know what the animal *is* and what it will take to keep it alive and evolving in the place it lives. In terms of conservation, these facts should be sufficient. At the time, I assumed they *were* sufficient.

I considered the others night-drifting in the cage with me: Roland was there to gather facts; Stephanie was there because she used the crane to gather facts in the daylight and wanted to see how that would work in the dark; Vibeke was there to direct the investigation. If I was not essential to the gathering of fact and if I now suspected that the goal that had originally motivated me was irrelevant, what was my business in the gondola? Maybe I was there only as a result of my passion for animals and of the fact that I have a tendency to put myself beside myself. I get keen on something, want so much to do it myself, and end up wondering why for God's sake I have made this choice. Sometimes it's only a matter of causing myself a little uneasiness, a little nervousness. But in the gondola of the canopy crane I was rattled and scared and had been for nearly three hours. Why in Christ's name don't I desist? I had come up too high and was, as they say, way out of my depth. No observation, no fact was worth this. Let Roland and the other people who get paid for it, who make their reputations with it, bring in the data. I wanted down.

Roland had gotten over his initial elation and was coming to terms with the fact that the canopy crane might not be the express elevator to the doors of the animal kingdom. But he was hardly discouraged. Finally his spotlight came to rest on something, a patch of brilliant blue. The crane's gondola floated over to it. It didn't move. It was a sleeping bird, a blue cotinga, which is a source of national pride to Panamanians. It was about the size of an oriole, and its body feathers gave off pale blue luminescence, its wings a darker iridescence. It perched absolutely still for us to look at.

Within moments the spotlight caught something else close by, a heavy brown shape huddled in the fork of a high branch.

"What is it?"

"A sloth," Vibeke said. "A two-toed sloth, I believe."

"Three-toed," Roland corrected. "See that lighter patch on its back? That's a scent gland. Only the three-toed has the scent gland. Usually the patch is more orange-colored."

The strength of the spotlight beam was diminishing, and Roland tried to conserve the battery by splashing the light on the foliage in momentary intervals. The sloth and the blue cotinga were the only sightings for the night.

Occasionally someone stifled a yawn, and finally, to my immense relief, Stephanie suggested we call it a night. Vibeke radioed the instruction to Edwin, and the gondola floated toward the tower. A few more creaks and groans as the cage slid down past the top surfaces of the leaves and eventually met the concrete pad. It was nearly midnight when we off-loaded the spotting gear and safety equipment and started back up the creek bed.

I noticed Vibeke wasn't with us and looked back to see her waiting with a light at the bottom of the tower. Edwin was still a hundred feet up. The only visible indication of him was his white tank top showing against the dark as he made his way, rung by rung, down the scaffolding. The sight of the tiny white patch in the night gave me a moment of extreme acrophobia, more intense than any that night. I had been too preoccupied with my own fear to worry about how exactly Edwin reached the crane cab. I had supposed he used a lift or some other mechanical device to get to the top of the crane. It never occurred to me that he would get to the top of the tower the same way he was now descending, rung by rung in the dark. It was his job. He would do what the scientists needed him to do. If his job for the animals was to lift the scientists up where they could see, what was my job for the animals? To stay below and tell the stories of their work, say why it's important to know what animals need to survive? Say how long it takes and what happens to the land in the meantime?

It turned out that Edwin would also, after changing back into his carefully kept town shirt, drive the truck back over the grueling forest road and rough highway that had brought us out to the crane. His capacities seemed extraordinary to me. He was a hero, a person who could get us back safe and sound to Gamboa. Once inside the truck, Stephanie fell asleep immediately, and shortly after her, Roland closed his eyes. In the front seat Vibeke seemed to struggle to stay alert. She nodded and jerked awake at the potholes. A very long night, but especially for Edwin. I worried that he would succumb to sleepiness like the rest of us—how long could you rightfully expect heroism to go on?—and I tried to keep a conversation going.

"Do you like riding out in the gondola?"

He was smiling. Evidently he hadn't heard my question.

"Edwin, do you ever get to take a ride in the gondola?"

Just the smile. After a moment Vibeke came awake long enough to say, "None of the crane drivers likes to go up in the basket. They think it's too scary."

8 ⬦ Predator and Parable

IT TAKES A LONG TIME TO GET THE DATA TO TELL THE STORY. It is a simple animal story: where the animal lives, how it reproduces, how it manages to get by. This story is what wins the animal scientific recognition, its ticket to go up into the Ark. When I left the burgeoning of rain forest species and the intensity of scientific activity in Panama, I had come to accept that the simple story the data tell is all that is necessary for conservation purposes. But only a few months later events made it clear that while the story that science tells is necessary, it is not sufficient because there are competing stories abroad. These competing stories drive persecution, to use the biologists' term, and they affect our willingness to safeguard the places animals live.

I heard from Roland that Diana, the little female coyote, had been killed. That autumn, just after the opening of bow-hunting season for deer, Dan Bogan had found her body under a tree stand. There was an arrow in it. Dan had managed to trap and collar ten coyotes, but they weren't surviving long enough for him to get any tracking information. He found them dead on the side of the road, the victims of Albany traffic. He found bodies of coyotes that he and Roland determined had been poisoned, and he found the corpses of two animals with bullets in them.

Why would anyone go to the trouble to kill these coyotes for no apparent purpose? Because what they know about the coyote has no basis in fact. What they know about almost any animal is not its data-driven story. It is a story driven by whatever stories people have been telling each other over the years. Coyotes dying in suburban Albany were a stark demonstration that what science's simple story has to cut through is a chaotic mix of irrationality and indifference. It is crucial that we recognize these confusions for what they are, because what we believe about an animal and what we believe about ourselves as animals have practical consequences for it. This is particularly true for mammalian predators. As Dan Bogan noted in his recent master's thesis, the main causes of predator die-out are persecution and habitat loss.

With the death of Diana, I began to listen more seriously to what my neighbors had to say on the subject of coyotes, and about that same time my friend Harry McCue told me a story I found both mystifying and instructive. Harry is an artist, well established in that line of work, and he also keeps sheep. Often the subjects of his prints and paintings are corners of his farm and details from the landscape around it on the ridge between Seneca and Cayuga lakes, much of it land classified by the tax assessor as "abandoned agricultural." His depictions of these places are tangled landscapes in which the line that represents a decaying apple tree can twist darkly to become a fragment of a gate. Something sinister works into his images. They could be violent if you let yourself think that way.

In person, Harry, a quiet, gentle person with heavy mustaches, gives no evidence of thinking this way, except for the reach of his deadpan humor. He told me he had a coyote family denning not far from the road in one of his hedgerows.

"What about your sheep?"

"The coyotes weren't bothering them," he said, "even though the den was just over near the fence line. But you know, the lambs were pretty big, and it was kind of fun watching the pups."

The coyotes were evidently habituated. They weren't disturbed by Harry's comings and goings among the sheep, and Harry said, "Sometimes I could see them all lying out there together." But this tranquil state of mutual observation was suddenly obliterated.

A neighbor pulled up into the yard. "Harry!" he called out magnanimously, "I shot those coyotes for you!"

Harry was dumbfounded.

"You didn't need them messin' around your sheep."

What Harry didn't need was his neighbor messing around with his gun.

The cause of this misunderstanding, I've discovered, was pretty typical of the mess of inconsistent attitudes about big carnivores and about coyotes in particular. It was a parable about our conflicting ideas about what's good for us and when it's good for us, a case in point about fear becoming violence.

The bow hunter who killed Diana had no use for her after he sent the arrow home. My guess is that he had been frustrated in his quest for a deer. So he just shot the first thing he came across before the sun set and ended the legal hunting day, then left his handiwork. No matter that it was, as Roland's e-mail pointed out, "perfectly legal." Diana's was the only legal killing.

"These people are taking *risks* to do this," Dan pointed out to me with what I thought rather naïve confidence in law enforcement. "One guy must have been shooting from right beside the road—and you're not allowed to fire a gun that close to a road—and one guy was in the city limits, closer than five hundred feet from a house, popping off out of season—it's all illegal. But he just popped off. Got the biggest coyote I ever caught, a great big male—Mars. Weighed about nineteen kilos [about forty-two pounds]."

Only one of the coyotes he had collared was still alive. But the man is patient. He kept up his solitary, disappointing work. He made his night rounds, tracking the one remaining coyote with a collar, and his daytime rounds, trying to trap more. If Dan was frustrated, he was reluctant to say so, and if he was discouraged, he was closemouthed about that too.

Some local wildlife watchers told Dan that they had heard the Albany landfill was a good place to see coyotes. Although he and Roland hadn't found much evidence in the coyote scat that the coyotes were eating garbage, he was ready to try just about anything. As a state employee, he was able to go through channels to get access to the dump and permission to trap there. I rode along with him and Roland on one of his daily track-checking runs.

Remarkably, the only part of the dump where the sweet, sick smell of garbage is strong is at the foot of the enormous hill of refuse, just beyond the gate where the trucks pull in. Otherwise the landfill seems like a small, grass-covered mountain with a dirt road almost as bad as the roads in Nahuelbuta winding up it and across its dome. Where the road stops just over the crest of the mountain, it looks down on a broad mowed slope that gives way to scrub growth and damp areas. This is the place where, Dan found, the coyotes come to play. He liked to drive to the top of the dump, turn off the truck, and wait for them to appear. It was a good spot for him and for the coyotes. "There aren't that many open grassy places like this one around here, and it's pretty quiet up here at night." He had set a few snares in the brush at the edge of the meadow but didn't seem to be able to catch any coyotes in them. At the time he wasn't aware that some of the locals thought the dump was also a playground for poachers.

From October through March every year, coyotes, along with the deer and fox and fisher that frequent the Pine Bush, but not the land-fill, are fair game for hunters and trappers. The New York State Department of Environmental Conservation has a management plan, and for animals whose numbers are sufficient—waterfowl, wild turkey, deer, fox, and coyote—there is a specified season. A good number of coyotes are legally shot or trapped, and because the trappers are successful, Roland and Dan have made an effort to get to know some of the men—and it is almost exclusively a rural, male pastime. They pride themselves on their understanding of the animals they kill—"you've got to learn to think like one of 'em, son," one older man told Dan when he paid a call, "*see* like one"—and they play by government rules.

"It's a cultural thing," Roland advised me about the trappers, "and they're dying out. Not many young guys are interested in keeping it up." I thought, No wonder—they get cold, wet, dirty, whether or not they catch anything, and they come home reeking of their bait. Who in the contemporary world would want to share quarters with a guy like this? But Roland's approach is trap and let trap. He and the trappers have a certain number of common interests, and the trappers know a lot. They furnish information, good stories, and carcasses. But their attitudes don't carry over into society at large.

This was a central finding of studies of public attitudes toward predators carried out by Yale sociologist Stephen Kellert after the first flush of environmentalism: the more you know about an animal, the more sympathy you have for it. Among a wide range of people in different parts of the United States, trappers scored highest on factual knowledge about animals, and they also expressed the most positive support of the animal. The early advocates for preserving land and animals were wealthy sportsmen like Teddy Roosevelt, and propelled by enlightened self-interest, the traditional alliance between blood sports and conservation continues.

I have to respect this alliance, and although I am constitutionally incapable of hunting myself, I should point out that there are any number of cases to be made for hunting. Informed hunting has its roots in human survival and probably, for the more reflective hunter, in the place of humans in the larger natural order. Regard for the natural world is what distinguishes the trigger-happy from the hunters. I dread the opening of deer season not because I will have to see gutted bucks draped over car roofs but because of all the ignorant yo-yos it will draw off the streets of Rochester and Syracuse, the kind of people who might shoot a coyote because it wandered under their stands when they hadn't been lucky enough for a deer to do the same.

These people carry what I think of as loose guns, guns that can't be accounted for by legitimate hunting, and they don't really know or care what goes on in the woods. They have been telling themselves the same story about coyotes over and over and listening to it. They have created their own parable of the coyote, and this is what makes it okay to shoot coyotes and leave the bodies, collared or uncollared, for the fisher or the buzzards.

J. Frank Dobie knew something about this parable. He tells the story of a young Englishman traveling by horseback through Colorado in 1846. By mistaken accounting, George Frederick Ruxton shot one more antelope than he and his party could use for their own food. This drew a wolf into a recurring encounter with Ruxton. "I had him twenty times a day within reach of my rifle, but we became such good friends, I never thought of molesting him." Dobie points out that "no American contemporary of Ruxton's on the frontier would have resisted killing that wolf. He would have said that he was killing it because the wolf killed; he would have said that the wolf was cruel, sneaking, cowardly. Actually he would have killed it because he was 'wrathy to kill.' It did not strike Ruxton that the wolf was cruel—at least no more cruel than man. It struck Ruxton that the wolf was interesting; he had towards it the sympathy that comes from civilized perspective."

What Dobie is onto is the demonization of predators and many furbearers in general that allows someone who pops off an animal like the coyote to feel righteous about the killing. Where I think Dobie wanders a little astray is in distinguishing the justification from the urge to kill, and then, straying a little further to conclude this urge is not part of the more sympathetic attitude cultivated in a civilized society. The urge is there all right, thriving in highly developed societies, stirred in with more recent ideas about animals as heroes—save the wolf, save the whale—and whatever more evenhanded ideas about natural systems have leached out from science and percolated up through the grade schools. In a sense, we are all "wrathy to kill." I rec-ognize it in the retired park ranger, a sweet and otherwise humane person, who hunts deer and turkey on our farm, and I recognize it even in myself. It is a primitive urge, and its sources are revulsion, fear, and a sense of entitlement.

Revulsion about carnivory is apparently antediluvian, if I read Genesis correctly. In directing Noah which animals to take aboard the Ark, God makes a distinction between clean and unclean animals: Noah was instructed to save from the floodwaters seven mating pairs of each clean animal and only one mating pair of each unclean ani-mal. Clean and unclean referred to ritual and diet, not to dirt or sex-ual habits. At the time Noah received his orders, the only foods pure enough for God's people were from plants, and the animals other than humans were divided between the clean—plant eaters accept-able for ritual sacrifice—and unclean, animals that ate the flesh of other animals, particularly those that ate their prey alive (also some that wriggled through life without legs, swam without fins, or had slimy skin). After the floodwaters receded, God qualified somewhat his thinking on the matter: his people, the same ones who had brought down his wrath and the Flood with their wickedness, were granted dominion over all the beasts and fishes, and "Every moving thing that liveth shall be meat for you; even as the green herb have I given you all things. But flesh with the life thereof, which is the blood thereof shall ye not eat."

Meat was now permitted, except for the flesh of a living animal or the flesh of an animal that ate live prey. The carnivores were still on God's list of the unclean, and I suspect to many nonscientists they still are. At some level, what they eat and how they eat it makes them dis-gusting to us—even though or perhaps because some of the items on their menus are also on ours. Furthermore, there is abundant evidence that at times what carnivores want to eat is, in fact, us. In this a little fear is healthy, a lack of it fatal—in fact, the evidence on humans killed by coyotes is that most of the killer coyotes were animals that had been getting handouts from people.

It is so easy to demonize these animals that even the people whose working lives are devoted to conserving them can slip into it. One day while we were rattling around the Pine Bush in Dan's antenna truck, he and Roland took delight in recounting for me the story of a man gone missing in the Adirondacks the previous winter. By the time his truck was found, any traces the man may have left were obscured by a number of snows. It was never determined exactly what happened to him, but his head was found on the ice in the middle of a lake, where the tracks around the head were evidence that the coyotes had been playing with it.

Something about the droll and rather offhand way they were telling all this made me suspect they were having fun with me.

"You guys expect me to go home and write all this down?"

"It was in the papers," Roland said.

"Yeah," Dan chimed in solemnly. "I saw it."

"If it had been fishers," Roland persisted, "they never would have found the guy's head."

"Yup. Just big weasels, and weasels go right for the brain."

"Remember that piece of flannel we found when we were doing stomach contents on that fisher the guy trapped up near the High Peaks?"

"Could have been a piece of the guy's shirt."

"Well," Roland pointed out the obvious, "it was a piece of *some-body's* shirt."

This line of thinking can become dissolute when somewhere in the processing of all the scary possibilities we're able to counter them with the conviction that we are in charge, we are rightfully in charge. We have been granted dominion over all the beasts, and if an animal is enough of a threat to challenge this order, we can off it. That's all it takes to put a person up where he or she rightfully belongs at the top of the biblical heap.

Until the 1930s, the demonization of predators was legitimized by both federal and state laws that characterized many furbearing animals as vermin and encouraged their extermination. The 1933 publication of Aldo Leopold's *Game Management* promoted emerging ideas about the need to balance wildlife populations and recognized the value of predators in this process. Three years later, a federal law, the Pittman-Robertson Act, established the financial wherewithal to begin working toward balance. Long before the 1930s, however, gray wolves, which are now succeeding quite well in a number of areas of the West, were eradicated from the eastern United States, including the Adirondack Park, an area three times the size of Greater Yellowstone. There are still a few gray wolves in eastern Canada, a strain Bob Wayne and his colleagues believe to be a coyote hybrid, like the red wolf, and in eastern Canada these wolves continue to be persecuted.

In the last few years, efforts to gain support for a reintroduction of the wolf in the Adirondacks have brought into high relief the attitudes that muddy our thinking about all carnivore predators. Many people in the Adirondacks have been perfectly content living in the absence of wolves, and they don't feel this absence as a lack. They don't like the idea of self-appointed outsiders trying to impose their notions of what's good for the woods in a patch of country they view as their own. As Kellert's surveys pointed out, they worry about the government imposing predators on them. Bringing wolves close to home is a scary idea, and "it's not going to happen any time soon," according to Roland, who has been gauging the level of public resistance.

I think the resistance, like wrathiness, is instructive. It's hard to welcome the prospect of wolves, real ones, large wild animals with sharp teeth, roaming freely near your house, hunting, killing what they will. It competes for our food, our stuff, our land. We are as territorial as the predators that worry us, and in our minds our territories are commodities. We "own" them. We buy and sell them. We defend them in court, and by rights, especially the right of dominion over the other animals, defend them from predators. I find it intriguing that the independent wealth that allowed Darwin to pursue his scientific investigations and the ideas that sprung from them came from some of the first paper mortgages to be issued in England.

People wouldn't have succeeded so well as a species if they hadn't been smart enough to secure safe places for themselves. Yet at the same time, over the past decade or so there has sprung up—even in the minds of many of the same people who do not want to have to deal with the realities of living wolves close to home—a romance of the wolf. In this story the wolf is a hero, a big, noble dog, with the power of nature itself, and a socially responsible mother or father just doing what's necessary to look out for the little ones back home in the den. This myth has grown up partly as a result of decades of work by biologists like Olaus Murie and David Mech that has made the wolf a more sympathetic character by detailing the complexities of its social life. That is, by making wolves seem more like us. In Kellert's attitude surveys of the 1980s, wolves were the most disliked wild animal, and although I'm sure the wolf biologists were hoping for some revamping of attitudes about wolves and top predators in general, I doubt what they had in mind was some of the tourist-trap, poster-in-the-bedroom responses to the rehabilitated wolf. Good-bye to the fangs and deceit of Little Red Riding Hood. Hello to Mowgli and his brothers. Hey, Pecos Bill.

We are of two minds about wolves and coyotes, and what is at work has to do with control. The wolf in Little Red Riding Hood, who is, of course, nameless, is beyond control in human territory, a loner who operates outside any society. Mowgli's wolf brothers are as tightly ordered as an army brigade. The coyotes who took in Pecos Bill gave him a strict upbringing and ethical education, and ironically part of this education included introducing Pecos Bill to the fearsome Wouser, a mythical hybrid monster that was half–mountain lion, half–grizzly bear, and the meanest critter in cowboy lit. We are comfortable with control, particularly when it comes to the places we think of as ours. For the most part, we are comfortable if we or someone like us is exerting control over our territory. Depending upon our point of view, wolves running loose in the Adirondacks are out of control, or releasing wolves in the park is returning control to the appropriate force, nature. (Of course, whether or not wolves should be reintroduced in the Adirondacks is also a question of biology, a question that is just as complicated as the attitudes behind the arguments and hasn't begun to be resolved.) There are irrational impulses at play in this debate because we are of two minds about any kind of conservation. We cling to myths and idealizations of animals and of nature, but we're not willing to cede enough control to live with the realities of animals and nature.

In the meantime, coyote is top dog in the Adirondacks and all over the East Coast, and I suspect if public attitudes were surveyed again, the coyote would take the honors once held by the wolf as most despised. He has introduced himself, and his romance isn't likely to shield him from wrathiness. If the guy who shot Mars were exposed he wouldn't be likely to experience any social disapproval, but a guy who shoots a wolf would likely be subject to outrage and speculation about whether or not he is a sociopath. The coyote romance ignores any wolflike nobleness he may have, ignores his speed, intelligence, and resilience. It focuses instead on his sneakiness and shiftlessness. Any meat in his mouth is ill-gotten gain.

I found that my friends and neighbors along the lake slope, many of whom are much better educated than I, held these general beliefs. Every story of a coyote sighting was accompanied by mention of wrongdoing by coyotes. "You know, they killed a calf up on the Hector grazing lands. At least that's what they said it was, coyotes." "Oh, you can see them sneaking around the old railroad bed just before dark, and the sound they make is really weird, like somebody deranged."

They seemed to know all this, and yet I also discovered that people who lived near me often saw coyotes without knowing what they were. One neighbor who lives close enough to our farm to see traffic from the coyotes that used our gorge as an expressway described an annoying dog that kept cutting across her vegetable garden. "It makes me worry about my cat."

"The cat old?"

"Fifteen, and he's blind."

"If I were you, Phyllis, I would keep the cat inside." It was best not to raise her fears—and along with them those of people all along the lake—about the presence of coyotes.

My neighbors and other people who think of coyotes as vermin that of necessity must be kept down by man might be surprised to learn that shooting is not the answer. Neither is trapping or poisoning or any other method of killing, because when the coyotes in a particular area are thinned out by human predation or disease, they respond by producing more pups. This has been documented by a number of studies carried out in the West for purposes of managing coyotes. When their numbers are strong and there is enough food and territory, the coyotes pack up and live more socially, hunting and possibly raising pups together. When their numbers are low, they are more solitary but during breeding season produce more litters and more pups. They respond to persecution like groundhogs: "Shoot one, and ten come to the funeral."

Our beliefs about wild animals and predators in particular are the results of parables created and re-created over the centuries, and it is no wonder that scientific knowledge of the same animals, so slow and difficult to come by, is also slow to enter the realm of belief. The two kinds of knowledge coexist in public consciousness. Our attitudes about predators and about land somehow ignore one of the central stories of science, evolution. Darwin's ideas about the emergence of progressively more sophisticated organisms always assumed that in the animal kingdom, humans were the end result, the animals at the end of the line. If we look at the story this theory tells as a parable, the lesson of that parable is humility. We humans have our place. We stand among the animals, somewhere near the apes. Darwin was very brave to put this idea out to the Victorian world. The humility this idea requires was hard to come by then, and in some quarters is still hard to come by.

Whether or not popular beliefs are accurate, what we believe about wild animals is a matter of more than parable. Not only can it impede conservation efforts—and the progress of the conservation Ark is already plenty slow due to the sluggish tide of data that propels it— but what we believe exerts pragmatic force on the lives of particular animals. My neighbors, and to some extent, I myself, act on the basis of what we think we know about coyotes and other animals in the wild. Our behavior—whether putting out syrup in a hummingbird feeder or the negligent slaughter of coyotes by car—affects their behavior, and as Roland pointed out to me about the coyotes and fishers of the Pine Bush, behavior and evolution are tightly linked reciprocal forces.

Darwin's journal observations of the tameness of the birds living on the Galápagos Islands—"a gun here is nearly superfluous"—are often cited as a demonstration of how the absence of threats from humans and other animals affects behavior and an animal's chances of surviving. A year and a half before Darwin landed on the Galápagos, the *Beagle* anchored in the Falkland Islands, where the young collector took particular notice of similar behavior in a "wolflike fox" and predicted its consequences for a carnivore he believed to be a discrete species. Earlier in that century, a Chilean commentator had described the animal as being the same species as the culpeo, the big, long-legged fox that travels through Nahuelbuta. "But," Darwin countered,

> I have seen both and they are quite distinct. These wolves are well known, from Byron's account of their tameness and curiosity; which the sailors, who ran into the water to avoid them,

mistook for fierceness. To this day their manners remain the same. They have been observed to enter a tent, and actually pull some meat from beneath the head of a sleeping seaman. The Gauchos, also, have frequently killed them in the evening, by holding out a piece of meat in one hand, and in the other a knife ready to stick them. . . . Their numbers have rapidly decreased. . . . Within a very few years after these islands shall have become regularly settled, in all probability, this fox will be classed with the dodo, as an animal which has perished from the face of the earth.

The so-called Falkland Islands wolf lasted another forty-five years and was declared extinct in 1880, while the scientist himself was still alive.

The Falkland Islands wolf had what wildlife management people refer to as "conflicts with humans." Today coyotes in the Northeast, because they often live in surprisingly tight quarters with people, adjust their comings and goings to avoid such conflict. This caution or timidity may not have always been true of coyotes. A number of nineteenth-century travelers in the West noticed great similarity between the dogs kept by Native Americans and the coyotes. "Beyond all question nothing more than a tamed coyote," declared one English naturalist, and the German duke Paul Wilhelm observed that "they seem to have been bred up originally from the coyote. They howl but do not bark; they growl and bristle up their hair; they approach quietly and bite without warning. They dislike Europeans especially." Evidently a nervous European gives off a scent different enough from a Plains Indian to incite coyote wrathiness—and, as any number of animal behaviorists have pointed out, it is impossible to study aggression in isolation from the reactions it elicits.

When they are as young as three weeks, eyes open and bumbling around the den, coyote pups begin training in both aggression and reaction. In the early 1970s, Marc Bekoff made highly detailed observations of captive coyote pups raised with their mother. Their play was an ongoing rehearsal of aggression beginning with one wobbly pup reaching out to slap the face of a littermate. As their strength and skills develop, the play fighting becomes more elaborate and rougher.

They roll and tumble, stand on each other, go belly up, bite each other's faces. Just like backyard puppies, except that, according to Bekoff, coyote pups play-fight more aggressively than domestic dogs or even wolves. At about five weeks, the wrestling turns serious, and the fights become real struggles to decide rank within the litter. Presiding over the snarling and hip slamming is the mother coyote, whose own fierce displays can cut the clowning in an instant.

We have a good sense of the indoctrination that goes on while the cubs are still nursing and staying close to the den. But when the weaning process begins and the pups begin to venture out with their mother, what transpires on these travels is more mysterious—perhaps one reason Dan was eager to get radio collars on pups. How does she educate them, and where does the information she imparts come from? Is it she who makes clear to them which elements in the new wide world are dangerous and to be avoided, and how did she learn this herself? What part of her teaching is the result of her own direct experience? And what part of her direct experience will shape the behavior of her pups' pups and the generations after?

With a few remarkable exceptions, which probably involve fatigue and hunger, the coyotes that live around me on the lake slope are shy and evasive. While I have often watched a red fox hunting in the open and fully aware of being observed, the coyotes run their errands in the interstices of the hedgerows and ravines. I often find fox scat along our paved road. The places I notice coyote scat are on dirt roads and tractor paths. The two animals are sharing the same terrain, the same weather, the same human neighbors, but the red fox is much more willing to risk an encounter with a human.

One day this spring, I drove around a corner near the village, and there on a grass-covered culvert was a red fox kit. I guessed its age at six to eight weeks. Its coat was pale red mottled with lighter tufts that it seemed to be shedding. It had a bright, humorous expression. I stopped the car, and it walked to the middle of the road to consider the vehicle. There was a car coming from the opposite direction. Teenage paint job, airfoils, and a thumping engine. I got out of my car and the kit looked a little worried but didn't quit his seat. So, thinking that the kid in the car might run down the kit but wouldn't run me over, I stepped into the other lane waving my arms. This was

too much for the young fox. He split—the only word for the speed of
this departure—for the culvert. The kid in the car didn't slow down,
just pulled around me in the wrong lane with a flash of middle finger.

On the same road in the same season of the year, I saw another
pup sitting in the tall grass on the shoulder of the road. It was gray
and fluffy, with dark shading on its lower legs and muzzle. I thought
it was some kind of shepherd-cross puppy. In the next seconds I decided that some jerk had dumped it on this country road, and I would
rescue it. My car was still a good distance away when I slowed down.
At the change in the engine sound, the puppy's head turned, and almost in the same motion, the little animal vanished. I had seen enough
to know it was a coyote pup. I went immediately to the spot where I
thought it had been sitting, and at first saw nothing but long spring
grass bordering heavy brambles. But there was faint trail threading
under the overhanging grass, too subtle to have been used by deer, and
there was no likely place on the other side of the road for them to cross
to. It was a path used by the coyotes to come to where they could sneak
a peak at the traffic and the people who took exercise along the road.
A good vantage point because it was easy to disappear from. Even if
the coyote pup didn't know what it was up against with the humans
along the road, it saw my car and knew the look of lethal danger.

One probable cause for this difference in the behavior of the two
cubs is that folks around here don't go in much for shooting foxes, but
as I have said, coyotes are fair game. It is possible that if we shot the
foxes as readily as we shoot the coyotes, they would become warier,
and sneakier. But we don't because what we believe about foxes is different from what we believe about coyotes.

Meanwhile, people like Roland and Dan keep working to bring in
the data. Dan Bogan was still on the job, trapping as doggedly as the
coyotes were avoiding him. Late one night just after Thanksgiving he
left his truck at the top of the dump to check a couple of snares. When
he returned to the truck, he found a note:

> Good job, asshole, 3 traps set, not in the least bit legal. No
> name or address on them. Probably a good idea not to, though,
> because if I knew who you were and where you lived, I would
> of beat the living shit out of you by now. . . . Tell you what—
> you just keep coming back to your little spot here and I'll catch

you mother fucker. P.S. If you do come back, make sure and bring your pistol with you, I'm gonna have mine.

Amazingly, Dan's response to this threat in the middle of the night in a high, lonely spot was to get back into the truck, close the door, and wait in the dark to see who showed up. No one did.

"It's probably not what you think, probably not as bad," Dan told me after enough time had passed so that he and the local DEC officer could begin to piece together the story. Although Dan had never encountered anyone else looking for animals around the dump, there was poaching of all kinds going on there at night. People in the neighborhood were concerned about it and suspected it involved the truck that drove up there so regularly, Dan's truck. Apparently the author of the note was one of the concerned neighbors.

"So really," Dan said about his prospective attacker, whose attitudes about wild animals were only slightly more confused than most, "his heart was in the right place."

9 ⩓ Islands and Ignorance

OUR HEARTS—OR THE HEARTS OF MANY OF US—MAY BE IN the right place, but muddy thinking and messy attitudes have allowed time to get ahead of us and land to get away from wildlife. As I look back on the experiences of the scientists with whom I worked and the lessons I brought home about the two foxes, coyotes, and kinkajous, I find it necessary to look at the animals and the places they live quite differently than Darwin did. For him, the animals and the places were there in marvelous abundance and overwhelming variety, waiting to be discovered, charted, and classified. For me, the animals and places are there, and the task is to keep them there.

Persecution and the larger danger of habitat loss are the primary threats to foxes and coyotes and many animals in many families, orders, and classes. What links persecution and habitat loss is ignorance. I use *ignorance* in its unloaded sense, the nonpejorative way Roland uses *persecution* and *promiscuous:* lack of knowledge. Ignorance, in turn, begets indifference. The lack of knowledge that allowed a bow hunter to kill Diana and leave her body also spawns the indifference of many people toward the processes of land fragmentation and habitat degradation.

The role of science is to push back the limits of ignorance. I did not learn what I expected to learn about foxes and coyotes, about kinkajous. I did not, as David Macdonald put it, get under any of the animal's skin and learn what it is to *be* a fox or a coyote, a kinkajou. But as a bystander of science I returned home with a treasury of arm's-length facts that would have satisfied Darwin, along with the understanding that these facts are necessary to do the conservation job. I came to accept that as things stand now, if you want to get those facts, do that job, you may have to interfere with nature.

The facts are necessary. The techniques are necessary. But given ignorance and the attitudes it promotes, they are not sufficient. I can return to the projects in Santa Cruz, the Pine Bush, and Nahuelbuta and see that every category of inquiry except classification—food, social organization, territory—is dependent on land and place, and I have a new appreciation of the amount of time that field research consumes. A lot, and that is its limitation.

After spending nine years in a life study of the Channel Islands fox, Gary Roemer, working with relatively good funding, spent another three trying to figure out why the foxes on Santa Cruz were vanishing. In the last of those years, Santa Cruz Island was partitioned with a fence. Roland Kays spent three years trapping and tracking and at the end of that time had one radio-collared coyote generating data as it roamed the office parks and met its friends at the top of the landfill. Elise McMahon stretched a shoestring for three years to get the most basic facts about a probably endangered rare fox, and all the while heavy machinery was chipping away at the cordillera surrounding Nahuelbuta.

There are many wildlife research projects—the National Geographic Society alone has funded an average of more than 30 a year for the past ninety years, and at this writing in 2006, the National Science Foundation had at least 129 under way. These are slowly revealing the facts of existence for this animal or that. The work is arduous, tedious, and chancy. The process of data gathering is deliberate and the pace of publication equally plodding. In the meantime, the animals are, quite literally, losing ground.

While the kinkajou lives in rain forest luxury that sprawls over Central America and northern South America, the foxes and coyotes whose stories were told here live on land fragments, islands, or *islas virtuales:* Santa Cruz, Chiloé, Nahuelbuta, and fragments of the Pine Bush. The deaths of Diana and the other radio-collared coyotes have made me try to understand the interplay between the isolation of these fragments, fact, and ignorance.

Historically, islands have been rich sources of inspiration and discovery for the natural sciences because they confine and concentrate natural events. The plants and animals on an island cannot escape the piece of land where they originate, and so the effects of the island's weather, terrain, water supply, and microbial culture are distilled as they regenerate. Darwin was interested in the influence of an island's isolation on its "productions." Although he made significant collections of these productions in the Galápagos and elsewhere, he did not immediately understand the evolutionary force they exerted but for a number of years turned over in his mind the possibilities, like these recorded in a telegraphic notebook entry:

> on separate islands ought to become different if kept long
> enough apart, with slightly different circumstances; Now Gala-
> pagos tortoises, Mocking Birds; Falkland Fox—Chiloe, fox—
> Inglish and Irish Hare. As thus we believe species vary, in
> changing climate we ought to find representative species; this
> we do in South America closely approaching—but as they
> inosculate, we must suppose the change is effected at once—
> something like a variety is produced.

It was Darwin's contemporary Alfred Russel Wallace who connected the dots between islands and the occurrence on them of peculiar species. These observations propelled his own independently conceived theory of transmutation, which he outlined for copublication in 1858 with Darwin's first published statement of his theory of the same process. Wallace understood that, over the long term, islands are evolutionary pressure cookers, and this is why many scientists after him, including Jonathan Losos, the herpetologist who visited Kelly and me in Nahuelbuta, and Roland's friend Martin Wikelski, have tried to document how the forms and features of animals evolve in the intense confinement of an island.

But the flip side of an island's capacity to spawn and nurture new life forms over the long term is its tendency over the short term to concentrate vulnerability, and because we are busy creating new islands, it is the vulnerability of suddenly marooned populations that worries me.

The plight of the marooned populations was the crucial lesson of Gary Roemer's work on Santa Cruz Island. When the island's original top predator, the bald eagle, disappeared from it, the little fox that lived there became the top predator. At the same time, the hogs that had been introduced on the island prospered in its confinement, and their piglets drew yet another top predator, the golden eagle, which threatened the Santa Cruz foxes with extirpation. No one *knew* that an animal farmed on the mainland would go hog wild reproducing, and no one *knew* golden eagles would find it worthwhile to fly over the Santa Barbara Channel to kill pigs and, as side catch, foxes. But Santa Cruz multiplied the effects of this ignorance.

At this writing, there is a project under way on the island to reintroduce the bald eagle, to reestablish it as top predator. Will the bald eagle successfully replace the golden eagle? If so, what will happen to the foxes and the skunks? How will Santa Cruz multiply the unforeseen consequences of this strategy?

It's true that there are other Channel Islands with other populations of the fox, which could conceivably provide new starter stock. But in the case of the Darwin's fox, multiplication of ignorance could quickly yield a finite zero. The Darwin's has been Red Listed and so, metaphorically speaking, the fox has made it aboard the Ark. But in real-world terms, the Darwin's still lives on islands. All through the Central Valley, the ambitions of the Chileans were tearing up ground and trees and hillsides. Down on the plain around Angol, the bulldozers were busy. To the west of town, the machines were gnawing into the foothills and as far up the first rise of the cordillera as they were able to creep. Making the tedious ride up into the mountains in the *micro* a couple of times, I saw a long-necked excavator that, having laid bare a patch of mountain, teetered out over the edge to reach for one more tree. Pulp and charcoal. One more tree.

Although foxes of all species are supposedly protected anywhere they occur throughout Chile, Nahuelbuta has the terrain and the cover to draw and hold them in some concentration. It is twenty-six square kilometers of haven for foxes, both the Darwin's and the chilla, and it serves as a hospitable stopover for the big fox called the culpeo. Surrounded by the ravages of hurry-up development and agriculture, the park is an island, as surely as Chiloé, the other home for the Darwin's, is an island.

The Darwin's foxes in Nahuelbuta number fewer than 100, those on Chiloé about 250, and scattered populations elsewhere in Chile are estimated to be 260. In total, they add up to one of the lowest populations of canids, with one of the most limited distributions in the world, and the fox's homes are insular. Elise and Jaime Jiménez speculate that because of its older ancestor and the historical reach of the forest in southern Chile, the Darwin's fox once had a much broader range. This makes it likely that remnant populations of the fox still have a foothold in pockets of forest between Chiloé and Nahuelbuta. But by now, these patches of forests have also been isolated.

On the island of Nahuelbuta, an outbreak of distemper or rabies, or even a disease of mice or plants that makes hard times for the foxes and the pumas, is potentially devastating. Christian Muñoz-Donoso captured on video a vivid demonstration of this vulnerability while he was working in Nahuelbuta. Although he recorded the event covertly, Christian did not start out to do a hidden camera job. In Chile there is a television quiz program devoted to environmental issues, *Supersalvaje,* for which Christian did videography. Shortly after I met Elise and she was back in the park on crutches, the show's host, a poised young Chilean man named Fernando, arranged to come to Nahuelbuta to report on Proyecto Zorro. The parking lot foxes and Elise would star, and Christian would shoot the video.

The images he captured opened with a fairly standard interview setup, Elise and Fernando seated in sunshine in an open grassy area below the Piedra del Aguila. Not far away, the parking lot foxes explored the possibilities of handouts without looking too beggarly, and against the backdrop of Nahuelbuta's boulders and dark stately araucarias, Christian's camera moved from the interview to the foxes to illustrate some point in the conversation. A few moments and the sound of an engine shattered the idyll. Elise's gaze lifted to a small white truck that pulled into the parking lot. She stared for a second and struggled up to her crutches.

The interview was lost, but Christian left the camera running. He knew her well enough to anticipate some kind of scene. Elise appeared beside the truck. The people inside it were blond Chilean hippies, a family or something, and with them they had two dogs. The parking lot foxes were unconcerned. Elise leaned in the window to explain in polite Spanish that no dogs were allowed in Nahuelbuta. The reason was that dogs carry diseases that could infect the foxes in the park—witness Papa coming over now to sniff the truck tires while the dogs in the car, long-legged piebald terriers, were barking frantically. A disease could wipe out the foxes. The head of the truck tribe, a lanky blond man with a thin ponytail, was not impressed by this information. He got out and left the door open so that a blonde woman and three blonde adolescent girls could step out into the parking lot. The door stood open for the dogs to jump out, and Elise raised her voice.

Then Fernando interposed his tactful presence in the picture, and the man, allowing the door to swing back so that it almost closed, disdainfully ignored Elise to explain to Fernando that she, being a *gringa,* both female and not native Chilean, could tell him nothing. The four women stood passively through the proceedings. They looked remarkably alike, and there was something not quite filial in the way the younger ones related to the tall man. They seemed to me an incestuous, stair-step harem. Fernando repeated man-to-man what Elise had already said, that while the new arrivals might not intend any harm to the wildlife in the park, his dogs posed a very real threat to the health of the foxes and all the other animals in the park.

Elise broke in. "Who let you into the park with those dogs?"

The guardaparques, apparently, if there was anyone at all tending the gate when the truck came through. The blond guy was getting impatient to be off. He motioned his women down the trail, and he went to the truck door. Elise was swearing big, broad Anglo-Saxon curses, and Fernando, caught in the crossfire, desisted. The outwardly impassive Christian amused himself with the whirring of the video-camera hanging innocently at his side.

The blond guy opened the truck door, and the terriers, yapping crazily, leaped to the ground, scrambling for Mama and Papa. The little foxes bolted, but for just a couple of steps. Then Mama turned on one of the dogs, snarling, snapping. The terrier drew back, and when Papa launched into the fray, the terriers tucked their tails and retreated down the trail after their strange family. Elise was still cussing. It may have been a rout, but if there were any damage to be done, it had been done. The dogs had come into physical contact with the foxes.

As the guardaparques' lack of vigilance at the park gates testifies, there is, in addition to outright ignorance, its close corollary indifference, the lack of effective understanding that causes slippage between what we know and how we act. This slippage is ubiquitous, and it is a fact to which Roland and Elise have both resigned themselves. Roland didn't hassle the poachers who invaded his research plot in Parque Nacional Soberanía. He knew they knew the rules, but he understood the circumstances under which they were getting by.

"Everybody cheats," Elise told me one day when I had been into the eastern part of the park and saw cattle grazing in a boggy meadow there. Then on the way back down the mountain to the VC I was pushed off the mucky trail by a troop of horses, apparently now resident, galloping in the same direction as I was traveling, ignoring the narrow log bridges and tearing through the muddy streambeds, excavating deep new crossings.

I returned to find Elise recharging her computer from the truck's battery. "I thought no livestock is allowed in Nahuelbuta," I said. "The horses seem to have the complete run of the place, and I saw a bunch of cows up near the Coimallin Road today."

"Happens all the time," she said. "They're from the campos around the park. In fact, some of them probably belong to the guardaparques. Everybody cheats. I don't think they necessarily mean to cheat. They know better, and their intentions are good. It's just that sometimes it's more convenient. Maybe the cattle push through the fence because there's more grass in the park, and it's more convenient to leave the fence down and let the cows get to the grass."

Elise doesn't protest these minor infractions, and somewhat contrary to her strong will, she usually swallows her opinions and tries to keep the social surfaces between her and the guardaparques smooth. She has to protect her position in the park, and she is there by the grace of CONAF, which employs the guardaparques. She has the long term in mind, the dream of building a research station in the park, and she can't afford to alienate the staff. So she saves her thunder. But my guess is that the guardaparques know it is there. The younger, happy-go-lucky ones who like to do wheelies on the government-issue motorbikes sober right up in Elise's presence.

"I had a fox killed last year. It had been mauled, and when I found it, the body was still warm. There was a guardaparque not too far away. I knew because I was working off the road, and I had seen him go by with his dog running loose beside the bike. I asked the guy if he knew the fox had been attacked, and he said he did. He said it looked like the work of another fox or maybe a puma. I pointed out that whatever killed the fox didn't eat it. I told him I'd seen his dog. He denied that he'd had the dog with him—that might have actually got him in trouble on the job—and of course, by now the dog had gone off somewhere. But I *knew* it was that dog, and a couple of hours later I saw his bike go by again, and the dog was right behind. So frustrating. I *knew* what had happened, and he knew that I knew. He knew that I was furious, but he also knew there wasn't anything else I could do. It would be his word against mine."

In the insular preserve of Nahuelbuta, she and the foxes were stuck with this cheating and its aftereffects. Of course, we don't know what those effects could be because we don't thoroughly understand the workings of *islas virtuales,* either the accidental ones or the ones we set aside as sanctuaries like Nahuelbuta. "These parks, these preserves— they are just big zoos," George Schaller pointed out to me, adding ruefully, "except that we haven't learned how to manage them."

It's important to recognize that science itself is not all-knowing, and ignorance visits even the scientist with the purest intentions. Misunderstanding of breeding dynamics—like the efforts to systematically cull coyotes in the West—uncalculated responses to predators, and unanticipated changes in food webs all love geographical isolation.

Scientific ignorance also attends relocations and reintroductions of wildlife. This country has experienced years of moving big carnivores around with only fairly shallow understanding of the results, and these have focused on determining the fate of the predators and the domestic livestock in the areas where the predators were released. Recently, however, research emphasis has shifted to the effects of reintroduced carnivores on naturally occurring prey populations in the territories they are retaking. One of these studies, led by Joel Berger at University of Nevada, looked at moose in Yellowstone, Sweden, and Norway in herds that had lived for fifty to a hundred years without the threat of grizzlies or wolves. They were what Berger called naïve moose, a term that still makes me smile.

The first breeding season after grizzlies and wolves returned to their home ranges, moose calves were killed in much greater numbers. But the female moose learned fairly rapidly to associate the odor of grizzly and wolf scat and the howling of wolves with danger and to move away from it. In successive seasons they were able to cut their calf losses. If adults had been killed at the same time as the calves—a distinct possibility with smaller herding animals—the devastation would have been greater and would have lasted longer. It could have become contemporary evidence for the Blitzkrieg hypothesis some paleontologists have offered about the extinctions of many large animals after the Ice Ages: these big, obvious targets were naïve. They didn't realize the diminutive humans were lethal, did nothing to protect or defend themselves, and were taken out by the scores. While it was fortunate that the naïve moose were quick learners, their case underscores the need to recognize the limitations of biology and to view wildlife management policies based on science with the same skepticism that drives research itself: Here is what we know. What is it that we don't know about it?

It is on islands where what we don't know hurts the worst—witness the fate of the tame Falkland Islands wolf, completely innocent of man. Recently, John Gittleman, the University of Virginia biologist who served as my mentor at the outset of this work, has been working on a series of mathematical simulations of extinction rates. In an article with Roland's friend Matt Gompper, he and Gompper point out that islands have been home to most of the mammals that have become extinct in the last five hundred years—the Falkland Islands wolf, the Tasmanian "tiger." At the same time, however, islands offer the opportunity to maximize human control, and so they are also the places selected for more than 60 percent of the reintroductions of carnivore predators. The dangers of this should be as evident as the advantages.

Unfortunately, we are creating new islands at a rapid clip. The land fragmentation and habitat degradation that result in these *islas virtuales* are abundantly evident. Many people witness them on a daily basis. Yet we have not made it a priority to address their dangers. We are indifferent because our attitudes about landholding are really no different, no more sophisticated, than those of animals living in the wild, especially carnivores and most particularly the big, charismatic, wide-roaming cats and dogs. Our self-interest is no more enlightened than the self-interest of animals in the so-called lower orders. We decide how much land we need. We mark our territory—rather than lift a leg on it, we use the currency of deeds and easements and rights of way—and we defend whatever piece of land we're claiming.

So the breakup proceeds, chunk by chunk or just crumbling around the edges. It eludes efforts to measure its extent or the extent of the breakage, partly because patchiness occurs naturally without assistance from humans, and changes in the size and shape of patches are difficult to delineate. Before European settlement of this country's lower forty-eight states, grasslands and shrublands took up about half the total land area, and forests accounted for the other half. Now each occupies about a third of the total land area and is continually shrinking. Forested land, for instance, has diminished by about 10 percent since the 1950s. At this writing about half of all natural lands—grass and shrublands, forests, and wetlands—consists of patches smaller than ten acres. Even so-called open land, which includes acreage that is farmed, is rapidly disintegrating. In the upstate counties surrounding Rochester, New York, 3½ acres of open land are lost for every birth or new arrival to the area.

In Chile the alteration of the landscape is ruder, even less hampered by policy, and more rapid. This is particularly true in the forest in the south of the country, where biologists have begun documenting the losses in bird species that accompany fragmentation. The implications for other animals, especially the larger, wider-ranging ones, are worrisome.

Science is long, land is short. The Ark has been slow to fill up. This troubles John Gittleman. "We need to find shortcuts," he said about getting sufficient information to protect wild animals and us from our ignorance. At an international meeting of mammalogists in London a few years ago, one scientist responded to this urgency with a proposal more serious than not that the most productive strategy would be for scientists to shift their efforts from detailed studies of individual species to working for preservation of tracts of land large enough to support healthy populations of all known mammals in a particular region. "That's why I work on big cats," Alan Rabinowitz told me, "the old umbrella species thing. If you can talk a government into setting aside enough land to support a tiger, then you've saved everything else that lives in its range." Obviously there are only so many big, charismatic cats with big territories to protect. This means that the scientists like Elise and Roland coming along behind Rabinowitz will be working to learn the more intricate lives of smaller animals and thereby setting up lines of defense for smaller tracts of land—and given the rate of fragmentation, this is well worth doing. If you can protect a piece of old forest in Chile, you're likely to have a Darwin's fox, and if you can defend remaining patches of pine barrens from strip malls and office complexes, you may get lucky and house a few coyotes.

Realistically, I don't see how we can wait for field biology to authorize every effort to protect the integrity of land areas sufficient to support wildlife. Although the public seems to need the outside authority that science provides, I think people like me—amateurs— need to apply the kind of skepticism that underlies science to both science and land development. We need to acknowledge that science is slow and imperfect and to take back some of the responsibility we seem to have handed off earlier to conservation biology. Rather than assume that an effort to disrupt a landscape is okay until proven not okay, those of us outside the conservation professions should assume that this alteration is not okay until proven otherwise. Somehow we need to put enough of a drag on land degradation to give wildlife management time to work through science—and to give the animals a chance.

We need to keep learning about the land and the animals we're trying to preserve, and the faster we learn it, the more effective our efforts will be. As studies done in the 1980s and my own experience make clear, the more you *know* about a wild animal, the more you *value* that animal. The Albany Pine Bush Preserve is positive evidence of this theory. It was created after the fact, after the suburbs had sprung up, and many of the sand hills have been bought up in antic- ipation of further development. What set the preservation process in motion was a small butterfly called the Karner blue. Science made it known that the butterfly was dying out, could soon be gone, and the Pine Bush was one of the very few places it could live. This prompted an awareness of the global rarity of the Pine Bush itself, the fact that there were only about twenty other patches of inland pine barrens in the world. Most of the open land there had been lost between 1940 and 1990, and even considering the rarity of the soils, pitch pine, and scrub oak, it seems remarkable that anyone would attempt to salvage the scraps of land around Albany. If the Adirondacks are an enormous island, and Nahuelbuta is an ordinary island, then the Pine Bush is a small archipelago. Its narrow fingers of sandy pine barrens intertwine with fingers of light industry, office buildings, shopping malls, and houses. It seems even more remarkable that mammals of any size con- tinue to pioneer in the preserve, but the animals that remain are the species that are not too discomfited by the presence of humans to ar- range their lives to accommodate our foibles. These are the survivors, the stubborn ones that are hardest to push out, and their viability is hardly assured, because although the Albany Pine Bush Commission has succeeded in slowly adding more than a hundred acres to the preserve over the past few years and has targeted many more acres for protection, the pressures of commercial development in the area are intense.

My observation that conservation biology is falling behind land consumption, which has already been voiced by any number of scientists, should not devalue long-term field studies of particular animals. This work holds its value. We need to continue to deepen our understanding of how things work in the woods. But in the meantime, we need to preserve the woods long enough to explore them carefully. In the end, as Kelly Cruce pointed out to me, this means changing the way people—all of us amateurs—think.

The day before Kelly left the park, she and I took the day shift and walked out into the park with the telemetry equipment. The day was unusual in that it started out bright and full of sun and it stayed that way. The only shadows in the park were in the denser stands of the old trees. Such a crystalline day was not one for foxes. They were laying low. It was to be expected and didn't trouble either of us. We walked and scanned for signals until midday, then picked out a sunny boulder where we could eat our sandwiches. Kelly shared her flask of tea with me, and we talked about her plans. She would return to the States long enough to get ready for the next assignment, a mist-net study of antbirds in Ecuador. And after that?

"I don't know. When I think about the time I've spent here, I think I've made a contribution. Maybe it's only one little fox in one little part of the world, but I think that means something, don't you? And this makes me say to myself it's time for me to run my own project, go to graduate school and learn how to run my own research project—I like the carnivores but I also like the birds, so maybe ornithology.

"Then I look around the park, I look around Chile, and I can see that the real solutions have to do with people. The way to really help conserve nature is to do something political, isn't it? It's all politics."

We slid down the boulder and were off again. I said, "Whatever you do, I hope you won't go back to *him*"—the subject of several miles of night hiking—and she laughed. The day was too bright for such a dark possibility.

With good footing and not much coming in on the radio, we were able to make good distance. We hiked out of the araucarias, through older stands of deciduous trees I never learned the names of, and higher up into young growth, trees with trunks growing thick enough to begin to shade out competing saplings. Suddenly sunlight took over again. There were no trees, just raw, open ground punctuated by boulders and a few charred trunks and strewn haphazardly with rotting logs and unexplainable scraps of sheet metal. Two strands of barbed wire were pressed into the ground in front of us. I followed Kelly across what was left of the fence, a little bewildered. "What is this? Where are we?"

"Oh, right," she said, realizing I'd never walked this far out from the VC with her. "It's the end of the park."

A Note on Published Sources

The motivating idea for this book germinated from my misreading of *The Snow Leopard* (New York: Viking Press, 1978; Penguin Books, 1996), Peter Matthiessen's luminous account of his trek into the Himalaya with George Schaller's biological expedition to study the "blue sheep." Both Matthiessen and Schaller hoped that in addition to learning the habits of the blue sheep, they would catch sight of the rare and elusive snow leopard. I read the book thirty years ago and at the time was so transported by the objects of their journey, the snow leopard and the "sheep" (which actually turn out to belong to the goat antelope family) that, until I reread the book in preparation for writing this one, I failed to understand the account as Matthiessen's spiritual journey and emotional rebalancing. What was lost has been recovered, and I recommend this book to anyone who wants to understand the intersections of nature with the spiritual and the personal.

After *The Snow Leopard* came George Schaller's own books and those of other carnivore biologists. For background to the work of the scientists with whom I traveled, I relied most heavily on Schaller's *Serengeti Lion: A Study of Predator-Prey Relations* (Chicago: University of Chicago Press, 1972) and *Last Panda* (Chicago: University of Chicago Press, 1993); Alan Rabinowitz's *Jaguar: One Man's Struggle to Establish the World's First Jaguar Preserve* (Washington, Covelo, London: Island Press, 2000); David Macdonald's *Running with the Fox* (New York: Facts on File, 1987); and R. F. Ewer's encyclopedic reference, *The Carnivores* (Ithaca, New York: Cornell University Press, 1973). For the general reader, there is one book in this category that is too important to overlook—Alan Rabinowitz's *Beyond the Last Village* (Washington, Covelo, London: Island Press, 2001). I recommend this for its moving elucidation of the forces at work in the margins between human and animal existence.

Journal articles were an important source of information, and among the many authors of these were Marc Bekoff, Joel Berger, Scott Creel, Todd Fuller, J. R. Ginsberg, John Gittleman, Matthew Gompper, Warren Johnson, Jaime Jiménez, Roland Kays, Paul Leyhausen, David Macdonald, Jaime Rau, Justina Ray, Gary Roemer, Blaire Van Valkenburgh, Robert Wayne, and Rosie Woodroffe. Daniel Bogan's recent master's thesis on coyotes set straight many key facts of coyote life.

My knowledge of Francis Bacon is limited to scattered readings from his prodigious literary output, selections from various biographies, and *Francis Bacon: His Career and His Thought,* by Fulton H. Anderson (University of Southern California Press, 1962). The admonishments on inductive reasoning that appear in Chapter 4 are quoted from Bacon's *Thoughts and Conclusions,* 9.

In my discussion of biological classification, the description of the fiery nineteenth-century debate about classification is drawn from Toby A. Appel's *The Cuvier-Geoffroy Debate* (New York: Oxford University Press, 1987), and the Reverend Bachman's letter to his coauthor, John James Audubon, with advice on mammal species is quoted in Alice Ford's introduction to *Audubon's Animals: The Quadrupeds of North America* (New York: The Studio Publications, Thomas Crowell, 1951). The passages on repetition in evolution are based on *From DNA to Diversity: Molecular Genetics and the Evolution of Animal Design* by Sean B. Carrol, Jennifer K. Grenier, and Scott D. Weatherbee (Malden, Massachusetts: Blackwell, 2005). Those readers interested in the IUCN status of an animal or plant species should consult the organization's website: http://www.IUCN.org.

For telling comments on popular attitudes toward large predators and the lore of the coyote and for references to reports of coyotes by early travelers of the West, I am indebted to J. Frank Dobie's *Voice of the Coyote* (Boston: Little Brown, Co., 1949). Diverse books of children's stories and Native American animal lore are the sources for the tales of the coyote I recount.

Gary Roemer's pointed question about reading Darwin shamed me to start reading, and I have never stopped. My travels were enriched by Darwin's *Voyage of the Beagle: Journal of Researches,* edited by Janet Browne and Michael Neve (London: Penguin Books, 1989). Originally published in 1845, Darwin's account of his experiences and discoveries is still very entertaining reading, and I have quoted extensively from it. I have also drawn directly from *The Correspondence of Charles Darwin,* volumes 1 and 3, edited by Frederick Burkhardt and Sydney Smith (Cambridge: Cambridge University Press, 1985) and from *Charles Darwin's Notebooks, 1836–1844,* edited by Paul H. Barrett, Peter J. Gautry, Sandra Herbert, David Kohn, and Sydney Smith (Ithaca, New York: British Museum and Cornell University Press, 1987).

For anyone who would understand Darwin's ideas and influence, *On the Origin of Species* (originally published in 1859) is essential; a recent edition can be found in the volume *From So Simple a Beginning,* edited by Edward O. Wilson (New York: W. W. Norton & Company, 2006). This is the source of Darwin's remarks about the imperfection of the fossil record.

Readers who want to know more about this scientist's life should take up the comprehensive and levelheaded account by Janet Browne, *Charles Darwin* (New York: Alfred A. Knopf; volume 1, *Voyaging,* was published in 1995, and volume 2, *The Power of Place,* appeared in 2002). Her work sets Darwin in the richly detailed context of his family, Victorian culture and politics, and the development of science in the nineteenth century. For those who want to pursue the development of Darwin's theory of evolution in depth, I recommend Niles Eldredge's *Darwin: Discovering the Tree of Life* (New York: W. W. Norton & Company, 2005), particularly for its lively analysis of the "transmutation" notebooks.

The works I cite here only begin to approach Darwin. There are many other important works by and about him, and their number is so daunting that I can only advise the reader to do what I plan to do: keep reading.